REVELATION

Chapters 6—13

J. Vernon McGee

THOMAS NELSON PUBLISHERS

Nashville • Atlanta • London • Vancouver

Published in Nashville, Tennessee, by Thomas Nelson, Inc.

Scripture quotations are from the KING JAMES VERSION of the Bible

Library of Congress Cataloging-in-Publication Data

McGee, J. Vernon (John Vernon), 1904–1988
[Thru the Bible with J. Vernon McGee]
Thru the Bible commentary series / J. Vernon McGee.
p. cm.
Reprint. Originally published: Thru the Bible with J. Vernon McGee. 1975.
Includes bibliographical references.
ISBN 0-7852-1065-2 (TR)
ISBN 0-7852-1122-5 (NRM)
1. Bible—Commentaries. I. Title.
BS491.2.M37 1991
220.7'7—dc20

90–41340
CIP

PRINTED IN MEXICO

17 18 19 20 21 22 23 24 25 — 04 03 02

CONTENTS

REVELATION—Chapters 6—13

PREFACE

The radio broadcasts of the Thru the Bible Radio five-year program were transcribed, edited, and published first in single-volume paperbacks to accommodate the radio audience.

There has been a minimal amount of further editing for this publication. Therefore, these messages are not the word-for-word recording of the taped messages which went out over the air. The changes were necessary to accommodate a reading audience rather than a listening audience.

These are popular messages, prepared originally for a radio audience. They should not be considered a commentary on the entire Bible in any sense of that term. These messages are devoid of any attempt to present a theological or technical commentary on the Bible. Behind these messages is a great deal of research and study in order to interpret the Bible from a popular rather than from a scholarly (and too-often boring) viewpoint.

We have definitely and deliberately attempted "to put the cookies on the bottom shelf so that the kiddies could get them."

The fact that these messages have been translated into many languages for radio broadcasting and have been received with enthusiasm reveals the need for a simple teaching of the whole Bible for the masses of the world.

I am indebted to many people and to many sources for bringing this volume into existence. I should express my especial thanks to my secretary, Gertrude Cutler, who supervised the editorial work; to Dr. Elliott R. Cole, my associate, who handled all the detailed work with the publishers; and finally, to my wife Ruth for tenaciously encouraging me from the beginning to put my notes and messages into printed form.

Solomon wrote, ". . . of making many books there is no end; and much study is a weariness of the flesh" (Eccl. 12:12). On a sea of books that flood the marketplace, we launch this series of THRU THE BIBLE with the hope that it might draw many to the one Book, *The Bible*.

J. VERNON MCGEE

REVELATION

INTRODUCTION

As we begin this Book of Revelation, I have mingled feelings. I am actually running scared as we come to this, one of the great books in the Word of God. Candidly, I must also say that it is with great joy that I begin it. Let me explain why I say this.

It has long been my practice, when I need a time of relaxation, to read a mystery story, a detective story. I confess that mystery stories have been more or less a hobby of mine over the years.

I do not read much of Agatha Christie anymore for the very simple reason that I have read so many of hers that I can usually figure out who the killer is, who committed the murder. Now I read Dorothy Sayers. By the way, she is a Christian, and she gets a great deal of Scripture into her books. The unsaved are reading the Bible without realizing it. Anyway, I have always enjoyed mystery stories.

When I began my ministry, I was a single man, and on Sunday nights after the evening service, I would get into bed and read one of the mystery stories.

Well, about one o'clock in the morning I would get to the place where the heroine has been tied down to the railroad tracks by the villain, and old Number 77 is going to be coming along in about twenty minutes. She is in a desperate situation. I think that the hero is going to be able to get there and rescue her, but I find out that he is in that old warehouse down by the pier, tied to a chair under which is a stick of dynamite with the fuse already lighted! Well, I can't leave the hero and heroine at one o'clock in the morning in that kind of position. But, since it is time for me to turn over and go to sleep, I slip over to the final page. A different scene greets me there. I see the hero and the heroine sitting out in a yard. I see a lovely cottage encircled by a white picket fence. They are married now and have a little baby who is playing there on the lawn. What a wonderful, comfortable scene that is!

So I would just turn back to the place where I stopped reading, and I would say to the hero and heroine, "I don't know how you are going to get out of it, but I tell you this: It's going to work out all right."

My friend, I have a book in the Bible called the Book of the Revelation, and it tells me how this world scene is going to end. I will be frank to say that I get a little disturbed today when I see what is happening in the world. It is a dark picture as I look out at it, and I wonder how it is going to work out. Well, all I do is turn to the last book of the Bible, and when I begin to read there, I find that it's going to work out all right. Do you know that? Emerson said that *things* are in the saddle, and they ride mankind. It does look that way. In fact, it looks as if the Devil is having a high holiday in the world, and I think he is, but God is going to work it out. God Himself will gain control—in fact, He has never lost control—and He is moving to the time when He is going to place His Son, the Lord Jesus Christ, upon the throne of His universe down here. It does look dark now. I think that any person today who looks at the world situation and takes an optimistic view of it has something wrong with his thinking. The world is in a desperate condition. However, I'm no pessimist because I have the Book of Revelation, and I can say to every person who has trusted Christ, "Don't you worry. It's going to work out all right." My friend, the thing is going to come out with God on top. Therefore, I want to be with *Him*. As Calvin put it, "I would rather lose now and win later than to win now and lose later." I want to say to you, friend, that I am on the side that appears to be losing now, but we are going to win later. The reason I know this is because I have been reading the Book of Revelation. And I hope that you are going to read it with me.

As I have said, I approach the Book of Revelation with fear and trembling, not primarily because of a lack of competence on my part (although that may be self-evident), but many other factors enter into this feeling. First of all, there may be a lack of knowledge on the part of the readers. You see, the Book of Revelation is the sixty-sixth book of the Bible, and it comes last. This means that we need to know sixty-five other books before we get to this place. You need to have the background of a working knowledge of all the Bible that precedes it. You need to have a feel of the Scriptures as well as have the facts of the Scriptures in your mind.

There is a second factor that gives me a feeling of alarm as I enter this book. It is the contemporary climate into which we are giving these studies in Revelation. It is not primarily because of a skeptical and doubting age—although it is certainly that—but it is because of these dark and difficult and desperate days in which we live. We see the failure of leadership in every field—government, politics, science, education, military, and entertainment. Since the educators cannot control even their own campuses, how are they going to supply leadership for the world? Business is managed by tycoons. And the actors can be heard on the media talk programs. Listening to them for only a brief time reveals that they have nothing to say. They do a lot of talking, but they say nothing that is worthwhile. None of these groups or segments of our society have any solutions. They are failures in the realm of leadership. There is a glaring lack of leadership. There is no one to lead us out of this moral morass or out of the difficult and Laocoön-like problems which have us all tangled up. We are living in a very difficult time, my friend. In fact, I think that it is one of the worst in the history of the church.

Knowledgeable men have been saying some very interesting things about this present hour. Please note that I am not quoting from any preachers but from outstanding men in other walks of life.

Dr. Urey, from the University of Chicago, who worked on the atomic bomb, began an article several years ago in *Collier's* magazine by saying, "I am a frightened man, and I want to frighten you."

Dr. John R. Mott returned from a trip around the world and made the statement that this was "the most dangerous era the world has ever known." And he raised the question of where we are heading. Then he made this further statement, "When I think of human tragedy, as I saw it and felt it, of the Christian ideals sacrificed as they have been, the thought comes to me that *God is preparing the way for some immense direct action.*"

Chancellor Robert M. Hutchins, of the University of Chicago, gave many people a shock several years ago when he made the statement that "devoting our educational efforts to infants between six and twenty-one seems futile." And he added, "The world may not last long enough." He contended that for this reason we should begin adult education.

Winston Churchill said, "Time may be short."

Mr. Luce, the owner of *Life*, *Time*, and *Fortune* magazines, addressed a group of missionaries who were the first to return to their fields after the war. Speaking in San Francisco, he made the statement that when he was a boy, the son of a Presbyterian missionary in China, he and his father often discussed the premillennial coming of Christ, and he thought that all missionaries who believed in that teaching were inclined to be fanatical. And then Mr. Luce said, "I wonder if there wasn't something to that position after all."

It is very interesting to note that *The Christian Century* carried an article by Wesner Fallaw which said, "A function of the Christian is to make preparation for world's end."

Dr. Charles Beard, the American historian, said, "All over the world the thinkers and searchers who scan the horizon of the future are attempting to assess the values of civilization and speculating about its destiny."

Dr. William Yogt, in the *Road to Civilization*, wrote: "The handwriting on the wall of five continents now tells us that the Day of Judgment is at hand."

Dr. Raymond B. Fosdick, president of the Rockefeller Foundation, said, "To many ears comes the sound of the tramp of doom. Time is short."

H. G. Wells declared before he died, "This world is at the end of its tether. The end of everything we call life is close at hand."

General Douglas MacArthur said, "We have had our last chance."

Former president Dwight Eisenhower said, "Without a moral regeneration throughout the world there is no hope for us as we are going to disappear one day in the dust of an atomic explosion."

Dr. Nicholas Murray Butler, ex-president of Columbia University, said, "The end cannot be far distant."

To make the picture even more bleak, the modern church has no solutions for the problems of this hour in which we are living. There was a phenomenal growth in church membership, especially after World War II, but that took place for only a few years. The growth went from 20 percent of the population in 1884 to 35 percent of the population in 1959. That was the high point of Protestant church membership. And it would indicate the possibility of a church on fire for God. Then it had wealth and was building tremendous programs, but recently the church has begun to lose, and it certainly is not affecting the contemporary culture of the present hour.

As far back as 1958 the late David Lawrence wrote an editorial which he entitled "The 'Mess' in the World." He described it very accurately, but even he did not have a solution for it. As we look out at the world in this present hour, we see that it is really in a mess.

For a long time now men in high positions have looked into the future and have said that there is a great crisis coming. (I wonder what they would say if they lived in our day!) As a result of this foreboding, there has been a growing interest in the Book of Revelation.

Although good expositors differ on the details of the Book of Revelation, when it comes to the broad interpretation, there are four major systems. (Broadus lists seven theories of interpretation and Tregelles lists three.)

1. The *preterist* interpretation is that all of Revelation has been fulfilled in the past. It had to do with local references in John's day and with the days of either Nero or Domitian. This view was held by Renan and by most German scholars, also by Elliott. The purpose of the Book of Revelation was to bring comfort to the persecuted church and was written in symbols that the Christians of that period would understand.

Now let me say that it was for the comfort of God's people, and it has been that for all ages, but to hold the preterist interpretation means that you might as well take the Book of Revelation out of the Bible, as it has no meaning at all for the present hour. This viewpoint has been answered and, I think, relegated to the limbo of lost things.

2. The *historical* interpretation is that the fulfillment of Revelation is going on continuously in the history of the church, from John's day

to the present time. Well, I believe that there is a certain amount of truth in this as far as the seven churches are concerned, as we shall see, but beyond that, it is obvious that the Book of Revelation is prophetic.

3. The *historical-spiritualist* interpretation is a refinement of the historical theory and was advanced first by Sir William Ramsay. This theory states that the two beasts are imperial and provincial Rome and that the point of the book is to encourage Christians. According to this theory, Revelation has been largely fulfilled and contains only spiritual lessons for the church today.

The system we know today as amillennialism has, for the most part, adopted this view. It dissipates and defeats the purpose of the book. In the seminary of my denomination, I studied Revelation in both Greek and English from the standpoint of the amillennialist. It was amazing to see how the facts of the Revelation could be dissipated into thin air by just saying, "Well, these are symbols." But they never were able to tell us exactly what they were symbols *of*. That was their problem. The fact of the matter is that some very unusual interpretations arise from this viewpoint. One interpreter sees Luther and the Reformation in a symbol that to another student pictures the invention of the printing press! In my opinion, interpretations of this type have hurt and defeated the purpose of the Book of Revelation.

4. The *futurist* interpretation is the view which is held by all premillennialists and is the one which I accept and present to you. It sees the Book of Revelation as primarily prophetic. Most premillennialists follow a certain form of interpretation that conforms to the Book of Revelation. (We will see this in the outline of the book.) It begins with the revelation of the glorified Christ. Then the church is brought before us, and the whole history of the church is given. Then, at the end of chapter 3, the church goes to heaven and we see it, not as the church anymore, but as the bride which will come to the earth with Christ when He comes to establish His kingdom—that thousand-year reign that John will tell us about. It will be a time of testing, for at the end of that period Satan will be released for a brief season. Then the final rebellion is put down and eternity begins. This is the viewpoint of Revelation which is generally accepted.

In our day there are many critics of this interpretation who not only attempt to discount it but say rather harsh things about it. One recent book of criticism, written by a layman, quotes me as being unable to answer his argument. Well, the fact of the matter is that he called me at home one morning as I was getting ready to go to my office. I wasn't well at the time, and I didn't want to get involved in an argument with a man who obviously was very fanatical in his position. In his book he makes the statement that I was *unable* to answer his question. If he misquotes the other Bible expositors as he misquotes me, I would have no confidence in his book whatsoever.

In his book he maintains that the premillennial futurist viewpoint is something that is brand new. I'll admit that it has been fully developed, as have all these other interpretations, during the past few years. When I was a young man and a new Christian, I was introduced to the theory known as postmillennialism. The postmillennialists believed that the world would get better and better, that the church would convert the whole world, and then Christ would come and reign. Well, that viewpoint is almost dead today. After two world wars, a worldwide depression, and the crises through which the world is passing, there are very few who still hold that viewpoint. By the time I enrolled in the seminary of my denomination, every professor was an amillennialist, that is, they didn't believe in a Millennium. It was to that view that most of the postmillennialists ran for cover. There was one professor in the seminary who was still a postmillennialist. He was very old and hard of hearing. In fact, when they told him that the war was over, he thought they meant the Civil War. He was really a back number, and he was still a postmillennialist.

At the risk of being a little tedious, I am going to give you the viewpoints of many men in the past to demonstrate that they were looking for Christ to return. They were not looking for the Great Tribulation, they were not even looking for the Millennium, but they were looking for *Him* to come. This expectation is the very heart of the premillennial viewpoint as we hold it today.

Barnabas, who was a co-worker with the apostle Paul, has been quoted as saying, "The true Sabbath is the one thousand years . . . when Christ comes back to reign."

Clement (A.D. 96), Bishop of Rome, said, "Let us every hour expect the kingdom of God . . . we know not the day."

Polycarp (A.D. 108), Bishop of Smyrna and finally burned at the stake there, said, "He will raise us from the dead . . . we shall . . . reign with Him."

Ignatius, Bishop of Antioch, who the historian Eusebius says was the apostle Peter's successor, commented, "Consider the times and expect Him."

Papias (A.D. 116), Bishop of Hierapolis, who—according to Irenaeus—saw and heard the apostle John, said, "There will be one thousand years . . . when the reign of Christ personally will be established on earth."

Justin Martyr (A.D. 150) said, "I and all others who are orthodox Christians, on all points, know there will be a thousand years in Jerusalem . . . as Isaiah and Ezekiel declared."

Irenaeus (A.D. 175), Bishop of Lyons, commenting on Jesus' promise to drink again of the fruit of the vine in His Father's kingdom, argues: "That this . . . can only be fulfilled upon our Lord's personal return to earth."

Tertullian (A.D. 200) said, "We do indeed confess that a kingdom is promised on earth."

Martin Luther said, "Let us not think that the coming of Christ is far off."

John Calvin, in his third book of *Institutes,* wrote: "Scripture uniformly enjoins us to look with expectation for the advent of Christ."

Canon A. R. Fausset said this: "The early Christian fathers, Clement, Ignatius, Justin Martyr, and Irenaeus, looked for the Lord's speedy return as the necessary precursor of the millennial kingdom. Not until the professing Church lost her first love, and became the harlot resting on the world power, did she cease to be the Bride going forth to meet the Bridegroom, and seek to reign already on earth without waiting for His Advent."

Dr. Elliott wrote: "All primitive expositors, except Origen and the few who rejected Revelation, were premillennial."

Gussler's work on church history says of this blessed hope that "it was so distinctly and prominently mentioned that we do not hesitate in regarding it as the general belief of that age."

Chillingworth declared: "It was the doctrine believed and taught by the most eminent fathers of the age next to the apostles and by none of that age condemned."

Dr. Adolf von Harnack wrote: "The earlier fathers—Irenaeus, Hippolytus, Tertullian, etc.—believed it because it was part of the tradition of the early church. It is the same all through the third and fourth centuries with those Latin theologians who escaped the influence of Greek speculation."

My friend, I have quoted these many men of the past as proof of the fact that from the days of the apostles and through the church of the first centuries the interpretation of the Scriptures was premillennial. When someone makes the statement that premillennialism is something that originated one hundred years ago with an old witch in England, he doesn't know what he is talking about. It is interesting to note that premillennialism was the belief of these very outstanding men of the early church.

There are six striking and singular features about the Book of Revelation.

1. It is the only prophetic book in the New Testament. There are seventeen prophetic books in the Old Testament and only this one in the New Testament.

2. John, the writer, reaches farther back into eternity past than does any other writer in Scripture. He does this in his Gospel which opens with this: "In the beginning was the Word, and the Word was with God, and the Word was God" (John 1:1). Then he moves up to the time of creation: "All things were made by him; and without him was not any thing made that was made" (John 1:3). Then, when John writes the Book of Revelation, he reaches farther on into eternity future and the eternal kingdom of our Lord and Savior Jesus Christ.

3. There is a special blessing which is promised to the readers of this book: "Blessed is he that readeth, and they that hear the words of this prophecy, and keep those things which are written therein: for the time is at hand" (Rev. 1:3). It is a blessing *promise*. Also, there is a

warning given at the end of the book issued to those who tamper with its contents: "For I testify unto every man that heareth the words of the prophecy of this book, If any man shall add unto these things, God shall add unto him the plagues that are written in this book: and if any man shall take away from the words of the book of this prophecy, God shall take away his part out of the book of life, and out of the holy city, and from the things which are written in this book" (Rev. 22:18–19). That warning ought to make these wild and weird interpreters of prophecy stop, look, and listen. It is dangerous to say just *anything* relative to the Book of Revelation because people today realize that we have come to a great crisis in history. To say something that is entirely out of line is to mislead them. Unfortunately, the most popular prophetic teachers in our day are those who have gone out on a limb. This has raised a very serious problem, and later on we will have repercussions from it.

4. It is not a *sealed* book. Daniel was told to seal the book until the time of the end (see Dan. 12:9), but John is told: "Seal not the sayings of the prophecy of this book: for the time is at hand" (Rev. 22:10). To say that the Book of Revelation is a jumble and impossible to make heads or tails out of and cannot be understood is to contradict this. It is not a sealed book. In fact, it is probably the best organized book in the Bible.

5. It is a series of visions expressed in symbols which deal with *reality*. The literal interpretation is always preferred unless John makes it clear that it is otherwise.

6. It is like a great union station where the great trunk lines of prophecy have come in from other portions of Scripture. Revelation does not originate or begin anything. Rather it consummates and concludes that which has been begun somewhere else in Scripture. It is imperative to a right understanding of the book to be able to trace each great subject of prophecy from the first reference to the terminal. There are at least ten great subjects of prophecy which find their consummation here. This is the reason that a knowledge of the rest of the Bible is imperative to an understanding of the Book of Revelation. It is calculated that there are over five hundred references or allusions to

the Old Testament in Revelation and that, of its 404 verses, 278 contain references to the Old Testament. In other words, over half of this book depends upon your understanding of the Old Testament.

Let's look at the Book of Revelation as an airport with ten great airlines coming into it. We need to understand where each began and how it was developed as it comes into the Book of Revelation. The ten great subjects of prophecy which find their consummation here are these:

1. The Lord Jesus Christ. He is the subject of the book. The subject is not the beasts nor the bowls of wrath but the Sin-bearer. The first mention of Him is way back in Genesis 3:15, as the Seed of the woman.

2. The church does not begin in the Old Testament. It is first mentioned by the Lord Jesus in Matthew 16:18: "And I say also unto thee, That thou art Peter, and upon this rock I will build my church; and the gates of hell shall not prevail against it."

3. The resurrection and the translation of the saints (see John 14; 1 Thess. 4:13–18; 1 Cor. 15:51–52).

4. The Great Tribulation, spoken of back in Deuteronomy 4 where God says that His people would be in tribulation.

5. Satan and evil (see Ezek. 28:11–18).

6. The "man of sin" (see Ezek. 28:1–10).

7. The course and end of apostate Christendom (see Dan. 2:31–45; Matt. 13).

8. The beginning, course, and end of the "times of the Gentiles" (see Dan. 2:37–45; Luke 21:24). The Lord Jesus said that Jerusalem will be trodden down of the Gentiles until the Times of the Gentiles are fulfilled.

9. The second coming of Christ. According to Jude 14–15, Enoch spoke of that, which takes us back to the time of the Genesis record.

10. Israel's covenants, beginning with the covenant which God made with Abraham in Genesis 12:1–3. God promised Israel five things, and God says in Revelation that He will fulfill them all.

Now I want to make a positive statement: The Book of Revelation is *not* a difficult book. The liberal theologian has tried to make it a difficult book, and the amillennialist considers it a symbolic and hard-to-understand book. Even some of our premillennialists are trying to demonstrate that it is weird and wild.

Actually, it is the most *orderly* book in the Bible. And there is no reason to misunderstand it. This is what I mean: It divides itself. John puts down the instructions given to him by Christ: "Write the things which thou hast seen, and the things which are, and the things which shall be hereafter" (Rev. 1:19)—past, present, and future. Then we will find that the book further divides itself in series of sevens, and each division is as orderly as it possibly can be. You will find no other book in the Bible that divides itself like that.

To those who claim that it is all symbolic and beyond our understanding, I say that the Book of Revelation is to be taken literally. And when a symbol is used, it will be so stated. Also it will be symbolic of *reality*, and the reality will be more real than the symbol for the simple reason that John uses symbols to describe reality. In our study of the book, that is an all-important principle to follow. Let's allow the Revelation to say what it wants to say.

Therefore, we have no right to reach into the book and draw out of it some of the wonderful pictures that John describes for us and interpret them as taking place in our day. Some of them are symbolic, symbolic of reality, but not of a reality which is currently taking place.

The church is set before us in the figure of seven churches which were real churches in existence in John's day. I have visited the ruins of all seven of them and have spent many hours there. In fact, I have visited some of them on four occasions, and I would love to go back tomorrow. To examine the ruins and study the locality is a very wonderful experience. It has made these churches live for me, and I can see how John was speaking into local situations but also giving the history of the church as a whole.

Then after chapter 3, the church is not mentioned anymore. The church is not the subject again in the entire Book of the Revelation. You may ask, "Do you mean that the church goes out of business?" Well, it leaves the earth and goes to heaven, and there it appears as the bride of Christ. When we see her in the last part of Revelation, she is not the church but the bride.

Then beginning with chapter 4, everything is definitely in the future from our vantage point at the present time. So when anyone reaches in and pulls out a revelation—some vision about famine or wars or anything of that sort—it just does not fit into the picture of our day. We need to let John tell it like it is. In fact, we need to let the whole Bible speak to us like that—just let it say what it wants to say. The idea of making wild and weird interpretations is one of the reasons I enter this book with a feeling of fear.

It is interesting to note that the subject of prophecy is being developed in our day. The great doctrines of the church have been developed in certain historical periods. At first, it was the doctrine of the Scripture being the Word of God. This was followed by the doctrine of the person of Christ, known as Christology. Then the doctrine of soteriology, or salvation, was developed. And so it has been down through the years. Now you and I are living in a day when prophecy is really being developed, and we need to exercise care as to what and to whom we listen.

When the Pilgrims sailed for America, their pastor at Leyden reminded them, "The Lord has more truth yet to break forth from His Holy Word. . . . Luther and Calvin were great shining lights in their times, yet they penetrated not the whole counsel of God. . . . Be ready to receive whatever truth shall be made known to you from the written word of God." That, my friend, is very good advice because God is not revealing His truth by giving you a vision or a dream or a new religion. Therefore, we need to be very sure that all new truth comes from a correct interpretation of the *Word of God*.

As I have indicated, the twentieth century has witnessed a renewed interest in eschatology (the doctrine of last things) which we call prophecy. Especially since World War I, great strides have been made in this field. New light has fallen upon this phase of Scripture. All of this attention has focused the light of deeper study on the Book of Revelation.

In the notes which I have made on this book, I have attempted to avoid the pitfall of presenting something new and novel just for the sake of being different. Likewise, I have steered clear of repeating threadbare clichés. Many works on Revelation are merely carbon copies of other works. In my own library I have more commentaries on the Revelation than on any other book of the Bible, and most of them are almost *copies* of those that have preceded them.

Another danger we need to avoid is that of thinking that the Book of Revelation can be put on a chart. Although I myself have a chart and have used it in teaching, I will not be using it in this study. The reason is that if it includes all it should, it is so complicated that nobody will understand it. On the other hand, if it is so brief that it can be understood, it doesn't give enough information. I have several charts sent to me by different men in whom I have great confidence. One of them is so complicated that I need a chart to understand his chart! So, although I won't be using a chart, I will use the brief sketch below to attempt to simplify the different stages of the Revelation and also give the overall picture.

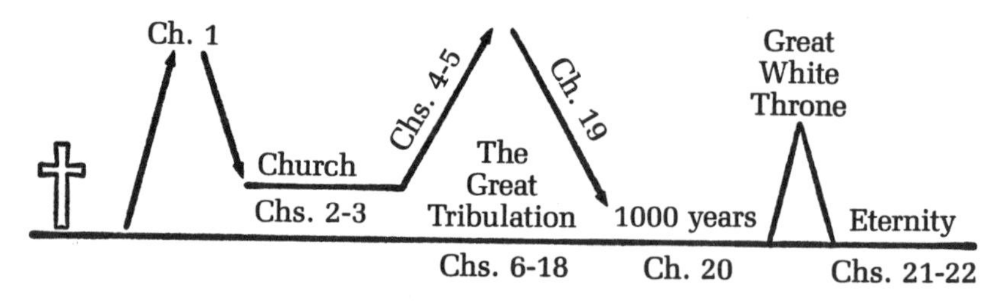

As you can see, it begins with the cross of Christ and His ascension. In chapter 1, we see the glorified Christ. In chapters 2—3 we see the church. In chapters 4—5 we see that the church is in heaven. Then on earth the Great Tribulation takes place, chapters 6—18. In chapter 19 we see that Christ returns to the earth and establishes His kingdom, and chapter 20 gives us the thousand-year reign of Christ. Then the Great White Throne is set up, the place where the lost are judged, and in chapters 21—22 eternity begins. That is the Book of Revelation.

Stauffer has made an important observation:

> Domitian was also the first emperor to wage a proper campaign against Christ, and the church answered the attack under the

leadership of Christ's last apostle, John of the Apocalypse. Nero had Paul and Peter destroyed, but he looked upon them as seditious Jews. Domitian was the first emperor to understand that behind the Christian movement there stood an enigmatic figure who threatened the glory of the emperors. He was the first to declare war on this figure, and the first also to lose the war—a foretaste of things to come.

The subject of this book is very important to see. To emphasize and reemphasize it, let me direct your attention to chapter 1, verse 1—"The Revelation of *Jesus Christ,* which God gave unto him, to shew unto his servants things which must shortly come to pass" (italics mine). Let's keep in mind that this book is a revelation of Jesus Christ. In the Gospels you see Him in the days of His flesh, but they do not give the full revelation of Jesus Christ. There you see Him in humiliation. Here in Revelation you see Him in glory. You see Him in charge of everything that takes place. He is in full command. This is the *unveiling* of Jesus Christ.

Snell has put it so well that I would like to quote him:

> In the Revelation the Lamb is the center around which all else is clustered, the foundation upon which everything lasting is built, the nail on which all hangs, the object to which all points, and the spring from which all blessing proceeds. The Lamb is the light, the glory, the life, the Lord of heaven and earth, from whose face all defilement must flee away, and in whose presence fullness of joy is known. Hence we cannot go far in the study of the Revelation without seeing the Lamb. Like direction posts along the road to remind us that He, who did by Himself purge our sins, is now highly exalted and that to Him every knee must bow and every tongue confess.

To that grand statement I say hallelujah! For the Lamb is going to reign upon this earth. That is God's intention, and that is God's purpose.

As I have said, the Book of Revelation is not really a difficult book. It divides itself very easily. This is one book that doesn't require our labor in making divisions in it. John does it all for us according to the instructions given to him. In verse 18 of the first chapter the Lord Jesus speaks as the glorified Christ: "I am he that liveth, and was dead; and, behold, I am alive for evermore, Amen; and have the keys of hell and of death." Notice the four grand statements He makes concerning Himself: "I am alive. I was dead. I am alive for evermore. And I have the keys of hell [the grave] and of death." Then He tells John to write, and He gives him his outline in chapter 1, verse 19: "Write the things which thou hast seen, and the things which are, and the things which shall be hereafter." My friend, this is a wonderful, grand division that He is giving. In fact, there is nothing quite like it.

He first says, "I am he that liveth." And He instructs John, "Write the things which thou hast seen." That is past tense, referring to the vision of the Son of Man in heaven, the glorified Christ in chapter 1.

Then He says, "I was dead, and, behold, I am alive." And His instruction is, "Write the things which are." This is present tense, referring to Christ's present ministry. We are going to see that the living Christ is very busy *doing* things today. Do you realize that He is the Head of the church? Do you know the reason the contemporary church is in such a mess? The reason is that the church is like a body that has been decapitated. It is no longer in touch with the Head of the church. We will see Christ's ministry to the church in chapters 2—3.

Thirdly, Christ said, "I have the keys of hell and of death." And when we get to chapter 5, we will see that no one could be found to open the book but one—the Lord Jesus Christ. So chapters 4—22 deal with the future, and Christ said to John, "Write the things that you are about to see after these things." It is very important to see that "after these things" is the Greek *meta tauta*. After what things? After the church things. So in chapters 4—22 he is dealing with things that are going to take place after the church leaves the earth. The fallacy of the hour is reaching into this third section and trying to pull those events up to the present. This gives rise to the wild and weird interpretations we hear in our day. Why don't we follow what John tells us? He gives us the past, present, and future of the Book of Revelation. He will let us know when he gets to the *meta tauta*, the "after these things." You can't miss it—unless you follow a system of interpretation that doesn't fit into the Book of Revelation.

As you will see by the outline that follows, I have used the divisions which John has given to us:

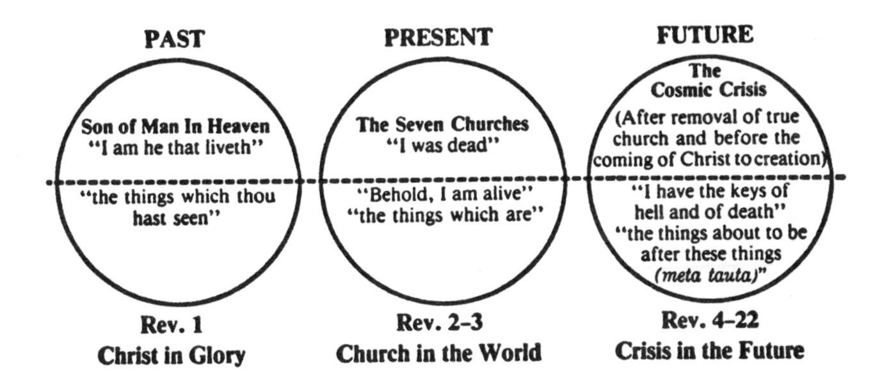

I. The *Person* of Jesus Christ—Christ in glory, chapter 1.
II. The *Possession* of Jesus Christ—the church in the world is His, chapters 2—3.
III. The *Program* of Jesus Christ—as seen in heaven, chapters 4—22.

The last section deals with the consummation of all things on this earth. This is what makes Revelation such a glorious and wonderful book.

In the first division of the Book of Revelation we will see the person of Christ in His position and glory as the Great High Priest who is in charge of His church. We will see that He is in absolute control. In the Gospels we find Him to be meek, lowly, and humble. He made Himself subject to His enemies on earth and died upon a cross! We find a completely different picture of Him in the Book of the Revelation. Here He is in absolute control. Although He is still the *Lamb* of God, it is His wrath that is revealed, the wrath of the Lamb, and it terrifies the earth. When He speaks in wrath, His judgment begins upon the earth.

The person of Jesus Christ is the theme of this book. When the scene moves to heaven, we see Him there, too, controlling everything. Not only in Revelation but in the entire Bible Jesus Christ is the major theme. The Scriptures are both theocentric and Christocentric, God-centered and Christ-centered. Since Christ is God, He is the One who fills the horizon of the total Word of God. This needs to be kept in mind in a special way as we study the Book of Revelation—even more than in the Gospels. The Bible as a whole tells us what He has done, what He is doing, and what He will do. The Book of Revelation emphasizes both what He *is doing* and what He *will do.*

The last book of the Old Testament, Malachi, closes with the mention of the Son of Righteousness which is yet to rise. It holds out a hope for a cursed earth, and that hope is the coming again of the Lord Jesus Christ. The Book of Revelation closes with the Bright and Morning Star, which is a figure of Christ at His coming to take the church out of the world. The Rapture is the hope of the New Testament, just as the revelation of Christ was the hope of the Old Testament. And the Book of Revelation will complete the revelation of Christ.

Notice also that there is a tie between Genesis and Revelation, the first and last books of the Bible. Genesis presents the beginning, and Revelation presents the end. Note the contrasts between the two books:

In Genesis the earth was created; in Revelation the earth passes away.

In Genesis was Satan's first rebellion; in Revelation is Satan's last rebellion.

In Genesis the sun, moon, and stars were for earth's government; in Revelation these same heavenly bodies are for earth's judgment. In Genesis the sun was to govern the day; in Revelation there is no need of the sun.

In Genesis darkness was called night; in Revelation there is "no night there" (see Rev. 21:25; 22:5).

In Genesis the waters were called seas; in Revelation there is no more sea.

In Genesis was the entrance of sin; in Revelation is the exodus of sin.

In Genesis the curse was pronounced; in Revelation the curse is removed.

In Genesis death entered; in Revelation there is no more death.

In Genesis was the beginning of sorrow and suffering; in Revelation there will be no more sorrow and no more tears.

In Genesis was the marriage of the first Adam; in Revelation is the marriage of the Last Adam.

In Genesis we saw man's city, Babylon, being built; in Revelation we see man's city, Babylon, destroyed and God's city, the New Jerusalem, brought into view.

In Genesis Satan's doom was pronounced; in Revelation Satan's doom is executed.

It is interesting that Genesis opens the Bible not only with a global view but also with a universal view—"In the beginning God created the heaven and the earth" (Gen. 1:1). And the Bible closes with another global and universal book. The Revelation shows what God is going to do with His universe and with His creatures. There is no other book quite like this.

OUTLINE

I. The Person of Jesus Christ—Christ in Glory, Chapter 1

A. Title of the Book, Chapter 1:1
B. Method of Revelation, Chapter 1:2
C. Beatitude of Bible Study, Chapter 1:3
D. Greetings from John the Writer and from Jesus Christ in Heaven, Chapter 1:4–8
E. The Post-Incarnate Christ in a Glorified Body, Judging His Church (the Great High Priest in the Holy of Holies), Chapter 1:9–18
"we know him no longer after the flesh"
F. Time Division of the Contents of Apocalypse, Chapter 1:19
G. Interpretation of the Seven Stars and Seven Lampstands, Chapter 1:20

II. The Possession of Jesus Christ—The Church in the World, Chapters 2—3

A. Letter of Christ to the Church in Ephesus, Chapter 2:1–7
B. Letter of Christ to the Church in Smyrna, Chapter 2:8–11
C. Letter of Christ to the Church in Pergamum, Chapter 2:12–17
D. Letter of Christ to the Church in Thyatira, Chapter 2:18–29
E. Letter of Christ to the Church in Sardis, Chapter 3:1–6
F. Letter of Christ to the Church in Philadelphia, Chapter 3:7–13
G. Letter of Christ to the Church in Laodicea, Chapter 3:14–22

III. The Program of Jesus Christ—The Scene in Heaven, Chapters 4—22

A. The Church in Heaven with Christ, Chapters 4—5
"I will come again, and receive you unto myself; that where I am there ye may be also"
1. Throne of God, Chapter 4:1–3
2. Twenty-four Elders, Chapter 4:4–5

3. Four Living Creatures, Chapter 4:6–11
4. Book with Seven Seals, Chapter 5:1–4
5. Christ: the Lion of the Tribe of Judah and the Lamb Which Has Been Slain, Chapter 5:5–10
6. Myriads of Angels of Heaven Join the Song of Praise and Redemption, Chapter 5:11–12
7. Universal Worship of the Savior and Sovereign of the Universe, Chapter 5:13–14

B. The Great Tribulation in the World, Chapters 6—18
   1. Opening of the Seven-Sealed Book, Chapters 6—8:1
      a. Opening of the First Seal, Chapter 6:1–2 (Rider on a White Horse)
      b. Opening of the Second Seal, Chapter 6:3–4 (Rider on a Red Horse)
      c. Opening of the Third Seal, Chapter 6:5–6 (Rider on a Black Horse)
      d. Opening of the Fourth Seal, Chapter 6:7–8 (Rider on a Pale Horse)
      e. Opening of the Fifth Seal, Chapter 6:9–11 (Prayer of the Martyred Remnant)
      f. Opening of the Sixth Seal, Chapter 6:12–17 (The Day of Wrath Has Come—Beginning the Last Half of the Great Tribulation)
      g. Interlude, Chapter 7
         (1) Reason for the Interlude between the 6th and 7th Seals, Chapter 7:1–3
         (2) Remnant of Israel Sealed, Chapter 7:4–8
         (3) Redeemed Multitude of Gentiles, Chapter 7:9–17
      h. Opening of the Seventh Seal—Introduction of Seven Trumpets, Chapter 8:1
   2. Blowing of the Seven Trumpets, Chapters 8:2—11:19
      a. Angel at the Altar with Censer of Incense, Chapter 8:2–6
      b. First Trumpet—Trees Burnt, Chapter 8:7
      c. Second Trumpet—Seas Become Blood, Chapter 8:8–9

d. Third Trumpet—Fresh Water Becomes Bitter, Chapter 8:10–11
e. Fourth Trumpet—Sun, Moon, Stars Smitten, Chapter 8:12–13
f. Fifth Trumpet—Fallen Star and Plague of Locusts, Chapter 9:1–12
g. Sixth Trumpet—Angels Loosed at River Euphrates, Chapter 9:13–21
h. Interlude between the Sixth and Seventh Trumpets, Chapters 10:1—11:14
   (1) The Strong Angel with the Little Book, Chapter 10:1–7
   (2) John Eats the Little Book, Chapter 10:8–11
   (3) Date for the Ending of "The Times of the Gentiles," Chapter 11:1–2
   (4) Duration of the Prophesying of the Two Witnesses, Chapter 11:3–12
   (5) Doom of the Second Woe—Great Earthquake, Chapter 11:13–14
i. Seventh Trumpet—End of Great Tribulation and Opening of Temple in Heaven, Chapter 11:15–19

3. Seven Performers During the Great Tribulation, Chapters 12—13
   a. The Woman—Israel, Chapter 12:1–2
   b. The Red Dragon—Satan, Chapter 12:3–4
   c. The Child of the Woman—Jesus Christ, Chapter 12:5–6
   d. Michael, the Archangel, Wars with the Dragon, Chapter 12:7–12
   e. The Dragon Persecutes the Woman, Chapter 12:13–16
   f. Remnant of Israel, Chapter 12:17
   g. Wild Beast Out of the Sea—a Political Power and a Person, Chapter 13:1–10
      (1) Wild Beast, Description, Chapter 13:1–2
      (2) Wild Beast, Death-Dealing Stroke, Chapter 13:3

(3) Wild Beast, Deity Assumed, Chapter 13:4–5
(4) Wild Beast, Defying God, Chapter 13:6–8
(5) Wild Beast, Defiance Denied to Anyone, Chapter 13:9–10

h. Wild Beast Out of the Earth—a Religious Leader, Chapter 13:11–18
(1) Wild Beast, Description, Chapter 13:11
(2) Wild Beast, Delegated Authority, Chapter 13:12–14
(3) Wild Beast, Delusion Perpetrated on the World, Chapter 13:15–17
(4) Wild Beast, Designation, Chapter 13:18

4. Looking to the End of the Great Tribulation, Chapter 14
a. Picture of the Lamb with the 144,000, Chapter 14:1–5
b. Proclamation of the Everlasting Gospel, Chapter 14:6–7
c. Pronouncement of Judgment on Babylon, Chapter 14:8
d. Pronouncement of Judgment on Those Who Received the Mark of the Beast, Chapter 14:9–12
e. Praise for Those Who Die in the Lord, Chapter 14:13
f. Preview of Armageddon, Chapter 14:14–20

5. Pouring Out of the Seven Mixing Bowls of Wrath, Chapters 15—16
a. Preparation for Final Judgment of the Great Tribulation, Chapters 15:1—16:1
(1) Tribulation Saints in Heaven Worship God Because He Is Holy and Just, Chapter 15:1–4
(2) Temple of the Tabernacle Opened in Heaven that Seven Angels, Having Seven Golden Bowls, Might Proceed Forth, Chapters 15:5—16:1

b. Pouring Out of the First Bowl, Chapter 16:2
c. Pouring Out of the Second Bowl, Chapter 16:3

- d. Pouring Out of the Third Bowl, Chapter 16:4–7
- e. Pouring Out of the Fourth Bowl, Chapter 16:8–9
- f. Pouring Out of the Fifth Bowl, Chapter 16:10–11
- g. Pouring Out of the Sixth Bowl, Chapter 16:12
- h. Interlude: Kings of Inhabited Earth Proceed to Har-Magedon, Chapter 16:13–16
- i. Pouring Out of the Seventh Bowl, Chapter 16:17–21

6. The Two Babylons Judged, Chapters 17—18
    - a. The Apostate Church in the Great Tribulation, Chapter 17
        - (1) Great Harlot Riding the Wild Beast, Chapter 17:1–7
        - (2) Wild Beast Destroys the Great Harlot, Chapter 17:8–18
    - b. Political and Commercial Babylon Judged, Chapter 18
        - (1) Announcement of Fall of Commercial and Political Babylon, Chapter 18:1–8
        - (2) Anguish in the World Because of Judgment on Babylon, Chapter 18:9–19
        - (3) Anticipation of Joy in Heaven Because of Judgment on Babylon, Chapter 18:20–24

C. Marriage of the Lamb and Return of Christ in Judgment, Chapter 19

1. Four Hallelujahs, Chapter 19:1–6
2. Bride of the Lamb and Marriage Supper, Chapter 19:7–10
3. Return of Christ as King of Kings and Lord of Lords, Chapter 19:11–16
4. Battle of Armageddon, Chapter 19:17–18
5. Hell Opened, Chapter 19:19–21

D. Millennium, Chapter 20

1. Satan Bound 1000 Years, Chapter 20:1–3
2. Saints of the Great Tribulation Reign with Christ 1000 Years, Chapter 20:4–6

3. Satan Loosed After 1000 Years, Chapter 20:7–9
4. Satan Cast into Lake of Fire and Brimstone, Chapter 20:10
5. Setting of Great White Throne Where Lost Are Judged and Follow Satan into Lake of Fire and Brimstone, Chapter 20:11–15

E. Entrance Into Eternity; Eternity Unveiled, Chapters 21—22
1. New Heaven, New Earth, New Jerusalem, Chapter 21:1–2
2. New Era, Chapter 21:3–8
3. New Jerusalem, Description of the Eternal Abode of the Bride, Chapter 21:9–21
4. New Relationship—God Dwelling with Man, Chapter 21:22–23
5. New Center of the New Creation, Chapter 21:24–27
6. River of Water of Life and Tree of Life, Chapter 22:1–5
7. Promise of Return of Christ, Chapter 22:6–16
8. Final Invitation and Warning, Chapter 22:17–19
9. Final Promise and Prayer, Chapter 22:20–21

CHAPTER 6

THEME: *Opening of the first six seals*

The sixth chapter of Revelation is the great watershed, the great divide, of the Book of Revelation. Here is a division that is all-important. Traveling on Highway 66 across northern New Mexico, you go through Albuquerque, then Gallup, to Winslow, Arizona, and up to Flagstaff. Somewhere in that area there is a place called the Continental Divide. I am told that you could drop a chip in a stream which is flowing on the west side of the divide, and it would end up in the Pacific Ocean, or you could put a chip in a stream on the east side of the divide, and it would eventually end up in the Atlantic Ocean by way of the Gulf of Mexico. This is a very important division which separates those two chips so that they find themselves worlds apart. We have such a great divide at chapter 6 of the Book of Revelation.

The third and final major division of Revelation began with chapter 4 where we found ourselves transferred to heaven. John was caught up to heaven, and we went right up with him and began to see things in heaven. However, we did not see anything labeled the church, because the church was the name given to it down here on the earth. But we did see the twenty-four elders. The elders had to get there some way—they were caught up, and they represent the church which will be at this time in heaven with Christ. From here on in the Book of Revelation, the church is no longer mentioned on the earth at all. There is an invitation at the end of the book which comes from the church, but that refers to this day in which we live.

You can see an orderly process in the Book of Revelation, and we need to follow Peter's rule for prophecy: "Knowing this first, that no prophecy of the scripture is of any private interpretation" (2 Pet. 1:20)—that is, you do not interpret any prophecy by itself. Each prophecy must be looked at as a part of a system and a program, and it must fit in with the others. By the time we get to the sixth chapter, a great many forget that John gave to us an orderly division of the Book of Revelation. John was told in Revelation 1:19, "Write [1] the things which thou hast seen"—that was that glorious vision of the glorified Christ as the Great High Priest amidst the lampstands, where He is keeping the light burning here upon the earth. [2] ". . . And the things which are"—that was the seven churches which represent the total earthly experience of the church from the Day of Pentecost to the *parousia,* from the Upper Room to the upper air, the total history of the church on earth. [3] ". . . And the things which shall be hereafter [*meta tauta*]." The earthly career of the church was ended in chapter 3. John said *meta tauta,* after these things, twice at the opening of chapter 4. He did that for the benefit of those who hold the historic viewpoint of Revelation, the amillennialists. Beginning, therefore, with chapter 4, John is showing us "the things which must be hereafter."

In chapters 4—5, we were in heaven with John. The first thing that we saw was a throne, and the Lord Jesus was there. He is the Lion of the tribe of Judah who is sitting at God's right hand, waiting until His enemies are to be made His footstool down here. He is also the Lamb, and we saw the emphasis upon His first coming. The Lamb, because He is the Redeemer, is the One who is able to take the seven-sealed book, which is the title deed of this earth.

Do you know that the Lord Jesus is the only One who is able to judge this earth? He is the One who is able to judge, not only because of who He is—He is God manifest in the flesh—but also because of what He has done. He created this earth, and that gives Him a right. He is worshiped in chapter 4 as the Creator. But then He also redeemed this earth, and in chapter 5 He is worshiped as the Redeemer. Since He is the Creator and the Redeemer, He is the only One worthy to judge this earth. He is the only One who is able to rule this earth. What a reflection upon the consummate conceit of little men down here who want to be judges! What right has the Supreme Court to judge anyone? What right has the Senate or the House of Representatives or the president to judge anyone? Who do they think they are? May I say to you, the Lord Jesus Christ alone is worthy to sit in judgment. Until one of these men can measure up to Him, he is not really in a position to judge in his own ability and strength. Any human judge who does not look to God is not worthy to sit on any bench and judge anyone. The injustice that is upon this earth today is brought about by little man sitting in judgment upon others. Jesus Christ is worthy. That is the picture that is given to us at the close of chapter 5.

OPENING OF THE SEVEN-SEALED BOOK

As we come to chapter 6, the scene shifts to the earth, and the question naturally is: What happens on the earth when the church leaves? The Great Tribulation takes place, and that is the subject of chapters 6—18. The opening of the seven-sealed book is the subject specifically of chapter 6 through verse 1 of chapter 8. These seven seals open up the Great Tribulation Period. The Lord Jesus breaks the seals, and the four horses ride forth. We will see the martyred dead during that period and the coming of the day of wrath. In a very orderly way, the seventh seal introduces the blowing of seven trumpets (see Rev. 8:2—11:19). The blowing of the seventh trumpet introduces seven startling persons (see Rev. 12—13). The beast out of the sea introduces the seven bowls of wrath (see Rev. 15—16). The last bowl of wrath brings to us the burden, or the judgment, of Babylon, and that brings to an end the Great Tribulation Period (see Rev. 17—18), and then Christ comes to the earth.

It is interesting to note that upon Babylon are the first and the last judgments. Babylon, at the Tower of Babel, represents the first organized rebellion against God (see Gen. 11:1–9). Babylon also represents the last rebellion against God, both religiously (see Rev. 17) and politically (see Rev. 18). This brings to an end man's little day on this earth.

The important thing for us to keep before us is the One who is worthy to open this book. He is directing everything now. As we were told at the beginning, this is the Revelation, the unveiling, of Jesus Christ. He is no longer walking among the lampstands, for they have all been removed from this earth. He is no longer the High Priest, standing as intercessor, but He is now the executor of God's will upon the earth as He opens the seals of the book. All the judgments of the Great Tribulation usher forth from the seals out of which come the trumpets, the persons, and the bowls.

The Great Tribulation is triggered from heaven. Jesus Christ directs the entire operation. This is the reason that Psalm 2:9 says, "Thou shalt break them with a rod of iron. . . ." Many will say that they don't like all this. Do you have a better suggestion as to how He should put down the rebellion on this earth? If you do, would you pass it on to the Lord Jesus? How do you think He should put it down? Suppose He came like He did more than nineteen hundred years ago. Do you think they are ready in Moscow, in the Kremlin, to turn authority over to Him? How about in any other country? How about in our country? I'm telling you, they are not about to turn it over to Him in Washington, D.C. Neither of our political parties is interested in putting Jesus Christ on the throne. They have some very unworthy men on both sides who would like to be on the throne. My friend, may I say to you that He *alone* is the One who is worthy. And how is He going to come to power? Exactly as the second psalm says: "Thou shalt break them with a rod of iron." We are going to see that taking place from now on in the Book of Revelation—this is judgment on the earth.

The church will be delivered from this period of judgment. Why? Is it because they are such nice, sweet, Sunday school children? Oh, no. They are sinners, but they are saved by the grace of God. Only those who reject the grace of God go into the Great Tribulation Period. This is my reason for believing that God has raised up the medium of radio in our day to get the Word of God out to the ends of the earth. He is going to let them all hear the gospel, and when they make their decision, that will decide whether or not they are going into the Great Tribulation.

Chapters 4—5 were but the preparation for that which was to follow—the judgment of the earth. In chapter 4 we saw the throne and the triune God; in chapter 5 we saw the book and the Lord Jesus Christ.

There are certain factors that are brought into focus which increase the intensity and the ferocity of the Great Tribulation:

1. The Holy Spirit will restrain evil no longer. Do I mean that He will leave the world? No, He won't leave. He was in the world before the Day of Pentecost, but on the Day of Pentecost He assumed a new ministry of baptizing believers into the body of Christ, a ministry of

indwelling them, of filling them, and of leading and guiding them in this world. He will take the church out of this world, but that does not mean that *He* is going to leave. He will still be here, but He will not restrain evil any longer. In other words, man is going to have his little day during that period, and so is Satan. This is the reason I don't want to be here.

2. The true church, as light and salt, will be gone from the earth. Although the church has very little influence in the world today, it still has a little, but when it leaves the earth, there will be none left.

3. The Devil knows that he has but a short time. He is going to make hay while the sun shines. He is going to take advantage of it during this period, and God is going to give him free rein.

4. Evil men will be free to carry out their nefarious plans. In other words, Antichrist will be able to take over this earth for a brief period of time.

5. There will be direct judgment from God. We see that here in v. 17, which says, "For the great day of his wrath is come; and who shall be able to stand?"

I do not think that the Great Tribulation breaks suddenly like a great tornado. The opening of the seals is gradual, logical, chronological. They are opened one at a time. The Book of Revelation makes sense, my friend.

As we come to the text of this chapter, may I make the statement very carefully that, from chapter 4 on, this is speaking of the future. Now if it is future and if we today are in the time of "the things which are," the period of the church, we cannot drag any of the seals, the trumpets, the bowls, or the persons up into our own day. I do believe we are seeing the setting of the stage, but I do not think that any of these things are taking place today. Yet we find that a great many persons are interpreting this section in just that way. It is sensationalism, of course, and I guess it gets listeners and sells books, but it surely isn't according to the way John put it down here. I simply want to lay it down as an axiom that from chapter 6 on it has reference to the future, and none of these things has come to pass as yet.

The section of Revelation which deals with the seven churches could be fitted into history, but you cannot fit any of this which follows into history. The difference between the two great systems of interpreting prophecy—the futurist and the historic viewpoints—really become manifest at this point in Revelation. The historical theory takes the position that all of this is history and can be fitted into history. It is quite interesting that many who hold the historical viewpoint assume that this is future from here on, or a little farther down they make it future—in other words, they just can't fit it into history. The amillennialist tends to fit everything from here on into history. As a result, there are about fifty different systems of interpretation, according to Dr. Walvoord, that have come out of the historical viewpoint. My friend, forty-nine of those are bound to be wrong, and personally, I think the other one is also wrong!

I went to a seminary that was amillennial, where they attempted to fit the rest of Revelation into the historical, or the amillennial, viewpoint. It became ridiculous and even comical at times. For example, when we reached the place where Scripture says that Satan was put into the bottomless pit, we were taught that that has already taken place. I asked the professor, "How do you explain the satanic activity that is taking place today?" He replied, "Satan is chained, but he has a long chain on him. It is like when you take a cow out into a vacant lot and tether her out on a long rope and let her graze." That was his explanation! And my comment was, "Doctor, I think Satan's got a pretty long chain on him then, because he is able to graze all over the world today!" It really makes some Scriptures seem rather ridiculous when you follow the historical viewpoint.

May I say very definitely that John has made it clear that we have now come to *future* things, and anything from here on through chapter 20 is still future. We are following a chronological order here, and it is very logical. You simply cannot say that these events are taking place today, and you cannot fit them into history.

OPENING OF THE FIRST SEAL—RIDER ON A WHITE HORSE

The Lord Jesus Christ takes the seven-sealed book, and He breaks the first seal.

And I saw when the Lamb opened one of the seals, and I heard, as it were the noise of thunder, one of the four beasts saying, Come and see.

And I saw, and behold a white horse: and he that sat on him had a bow; and a crown was given unto him: and he went forth conquering, and to conquer [Rev. 6:1–2].

Here is my own translation of these verses:

> *And I saw when the Lamb opened one of the seven seals, and I heard one of the four living creatures saying as a sound of thunder, Go. And I saw, and behold a white horse, and one sitting on him having a bow, and a crown was given to him, and he went out conquering, and to conquer.*

Christ is going to break all the seals, *ad seriatum*, right in order. He is in full charge, and every creature in heaven is moving at His command. So the four horsemen are now going to ride forth. He breaks the seal, and says, "Go." Although the King James Version gives the impression that an invitation is given to John to "Come and see," the phrase "and see" should be omitted, and since the order issues from heaven, the proper translation is "Go."

It is restated by John that he "saw" and he "heard." This is television that we are looking at.

Attempts to determine the symbolism of the rider on the white horse has given rise to many differences in opinion. The preponderate interpretation among commentators is that he represents Christ. They use Psalm 45 and Revelation 19 in support of their position. But most of the contemporary Bible expositors of the premillennial school say that the white horse and the rider is Antichrist. That is the position of Scott, Ironside, Chafer, Walvoord, Woodbridge and Pentecost. And it happens to be my position also. It would be pretty difficult for the Lord Jesus, who is the one opening the seals, now to make a quick change, mount a horse, and come riding forth.

To me that would be a rather inconsistent and unbelievable position. I personally take the viewpoint that this is Antichrist, this is an *imitation* of Christ, this is one who *pretends* to be Christ, who comes forth.

We are moving today in the direction of a world dictator. More and more is this true. All the nations of the world are disturbed. Lawlessness abounds, and governments are not able to control as they should. This is all preparing the way for the coming of one who is going to rule.

Antichrist does not appear as a villain. After all, Satan's angels are angels of light. He is not going to have horns or cloven feet. Rather, he is going to be the most attractive man the world has ever seen. They will elect him, and the world will acclaim him because he has come in his own name. But when he takes over, it sure is going to be bad for the world.

This is not just the ravings of a preacher here in California. This is something that other men in other walks of life, who apparently make no great claims to being Christians, have said. Professor A. J. Toynbee, Director of Studies in the Royal Institute of International Affairs, said:

> By forcing on mankind more and more lethal weapons and at the same time making the whole world more and more interdependent economically, technology has brought mankind to such a degree of distress that we are ripe for deifying any new Caesar who might succeed in giving the world unity and peace.

That will be the platform that Antichrist will come in on—world unity and peace. I think that if anybody appeared on the scene now and offered the world that, the world wouldn't ask whether he came from heaven or hell. I don't think they would care, because they want peace at any price, and we have spent billions of dollars trying to obtain it.

G. K. Chesterton observed in his day: "One of the paradoxes of this age is that it is the age of Pacifism, but not the age of Peace." There is a great deal of *talking* about peace.

In a news item some time ago, we read of a woman in Fayetteville, Arkansas, who named the United Nations as the beneficiary to her $700,000 estate "in the fervent hope that this relatively small contribution may be of some effect in bringing about universal peace on earth and good will among men." I want to say that she poured that money down a rat hole, because you are not going to buy peace with $700,000 or even millions of dollars. We have given away *billions* of dollars throughout the world, and we do not have peace.

The Ford Foundation, one of the world's wealthiest private organizations, has announced that their money eventually will be used to work for world peace and better government, living and education conditions—yet the world gets worse all the time.

When Antichrist comes to power, he is going to talk peace, and the world will think that it is entering the Millennium when it is actually entering the Great Tribulation. The Great Tribulation comes in like a lamb, but it goes out like a lion. A promise of peace is the big lie the world is going to believe.

This rider could not be Christ, therefore, in view of the fact that Christ is the Lamb in the midst of the throne who, as the Lion of the tribe of Judah, the Root of David, is directing these events from heaven and is giving the orders to the four horsemen to ride. Christ is *clearly* identified in Revelation 19, while here the identity is certainly obscure, which suggests that it is not Christ but an imitation of Him.

OPENING OF THE SECOND SEAL—RIDER ON A RED HORSE

And when he had opened the second seal, I heard the second beast say, Come and see.

And there went out another horse that was red: and power was given to him that sat thereon to take peace from the earth, and that they should kill one another: and there was given unto him a great sword [Rev. 6:3–4].

And when He opened the second seal, I heard the second living creature saying, Go. And another horse, fiery red (flame colored) went out. And there was given to the one sitting on him to take peace from the earth, and that they should kill (violently) one another, and there was given to him a great sword.

The first horseman could not be Christ, because when *He* brings peace to this earth, it is going to be permanent. This is a short-lived peace. Immediately after the white horse went forth, here comes the red horse of war on the earth. The peace which the rider on the white horse brought to the earth was temporary and counterfeit. The Antichrist presents himself as a ruler who brings peace to the world, but he cannot guarantee it, for God says, "There is no peace, saith my God, to the wicked" (Isa. 57:21). And that passage of Scripture certainly has been fulfilled.

Isn't peace exactly what every candidate for office in our country has promised? Certainly that has been true in my lifetime. I never shall forget the candidate who said that our boys would never again go across the ocean to fight. What baloney that was! We were promised peace, and every candidate since then has promised peace. One of them dropped two atom bombs, and immediately afterward we began to talk about peace. Every candidate since then—no exception and regardless of party—has said he was going to bring peace. My friend, we are as far from peace today as we have ever been. Already the clouds are gathering for World War III.

Antichrist will be a phony. He won't bring peace because here goes the fiery red horse of war riding throughout the earth again. And this is going to be a *real* world war. Don't say that this has been fulfilled—it hasn't been. It is future.

OPENING OF THE THIRD SEAL—RIDER ON A BLACK HORSE

And when he had opened the third seal, I heard the third beast say, Come and see. And I beheld, and lo a

black horse; and he that sat on him had a pair of balances in his hand.

And I heard a voice in the midst of the four beasts say, A measure of wheat for a penny, and three measures of barley for a penny; and see thou hurt not the oil and the wine [Rev. 6:5–6].

And when He had opened the third seal, I heard the third living creature saying, Go. And I saw, and behold a black horse, and the one sitting on him having a balance (scales) in his hand. And I heard a voice in the midst of the four living creatures say, a choenix (a quart) of wheat for a denarius, and three choenix (quarts) of barley for a denarius; and do not hurt the oil and the wine.

John again says, "I heard" and "I saw." He just wants to make sure that we know that. The color of the black horse indicates mourning (see Jer. 4:28; Mal. 3:14, "mournfully in black"), and it also speaks of famine. In Lamentations 4:8–9 we read: "Their visage is blacker than a coal; they are not known in the streets: their skin cleaveth to their bones; it is withered, it is become like a stick. They that be slain with the sword are better than they that be slain with hunger: for these pine away, stricken through for want of the fruits of the field."

The black horse represents the worldwide famine that is to come on the earth. Always after a war there is a shortage of foodstuff.

The Greek historian Herodotus says that a choenix (quart) of corn was a soldier's daily supply of food. A denarius was a day's wage (see Matt. 20:2). Therefore, a working man will be unable to support his family in that day.

The oil and the wine are luxuries that are enjoyed by the rich. Oil would correspond to our toiletries, the beauty aids and the body conditioners that we use today; that is, the luxuries of life. The wine corresponds to the liquor that will be in abundance. Isn't it interesting that there will not be enough foodstuff, not enough barley for food, but there will be enough barley to make liquor! They will make it in that day, and the rich are the ones who will get it.

Let me be very frank. During World War II the rich, for the most part, were able to get meat. They were able to get the luxuries of life. A very wealthy man told me that he never missed getting a big T-bone steak anytime that he wanted it. But I can remember getting very tired of eating tongue, which was one thing we didn't have to have blue chips to get and was something that was not rationed. In this day that is coming, things won't change. The rich are going to get theirs, but the poor won't be able to get theirs. That is the way it has always been. I feel like saying, "Ho hum," when I hear these sincere egg-headed boys talking about how they are going to work out the poverty problem. All that it has accomplished is that it has given a good job to a lot of *them*, but so far it hasn't filtered down and been a blessing to the poor. It has never helped the poor to lift themselves up with any degree of pride. Why? Because the only Man who can lift up the poor is Jesus Christ. None of these egg-headed boys is able to do it. I am sorry to have to say that, but somebody needs to speak out against all of this tomfoolery that our government is going through. All that this wasteful spending of money does is to create more bureaucracy and to sap our tax dollars. This is the sort of thing that is abroad today, but just think what it is going to be like in that future day. This which we are talking about in the Revelation is future. The only reason that I make application to today is to show that this is not unreasonable; it *is* going to take place.

Way back in 1798, the Rev. Thomas Malthus concluded that "the power of population is infinitely greater than the power of the earth to produce subsistence for man." His prediction had little weight in his day. In 1959 the United Nations' seventy-seven-nation Food and Agriculture Organization met in Rome to talk about "the fight against hunger and malnutrition." At this meeting Toynbee declared: "Sooner or later food production will reach its limit. And then, if population is still increasing, famine will do the execution that was done in the past by famine, pestilence and war combined." Sir John Boyd Orr, at one time the Director-General of the UN Food and Agriculture Organization, warned, "I shall finish my office by giving a last warning to the world. If it is not solved there will be world chaos in the next fifty years. The nations of the world are insane." Someone has reported, "There are today 750 million people getting hungrier in countries bordering the Communist sphere." This thing is growing, my friend. Famine always follows war.

OPENING OF THE FOURTH SEAL—RIDER ON A PALE HORSE

And when he had opened the fourth seal, I heard the voice of the fourth beast say, Come and see.

And I looked, and behold a pale horse: and his name that sat on him was Death, and Hell followed with him. And power was given unto them over the fourth part of the earth, to kill with sword, and with hunger, and with death, and with the beasts of the earth [Rev. 6:7–8].

And when He had opened the fourth seal, I heard the voice of the fourth living creature saying, Go. And I looked and behold a pale (greenish-yellow) horse; and the one sitting upon him, Death was his name; and Hades followed with him. And there was given unto them authority over the fourth part of the earth, to kill with the sword, and with famine, and with death (pestilence), and by the (wild) beasts of the earth.

Here is a pestilence that is going to take out one-fourth of the population of the earth. There will not be enough antibiotics and penicillin to go around in that day to stop it.

"Death was his name." Death is no more personalized here than is war—although the rider is given the name of death. There is more involved in physical death than meets the eye, for the human being is more than physical, and death is more than cessation of physical activity. While death takes the body, hades is the place where the spirit of a lost man goes (see Luke 16:23, ASV).

A literal translation of Romans 5:14 reads thus: "And nevertheless death became king from Adam down to Moses, even over them who did not sin after the fashion of Adam's sin [transgression] who is the type of Him [The Adam] who was to come [The Coming One]."

"Death was his name; and Hades followed with him." The word for *hades* is sometimes unfortunately translated by the word *hell* as in Luke 16:23 where, speaking of the rich man and Lazarus, we read: "And in hell he lift up his eyes, being in torments, and seeth Abraham afar off, and Lazarus in his bosom." *Hell* is a very unfortunate translation there; it is this same word *hades*, and actually, it does not refer to hell at all. It speaks of physical death—either where the spirit goes or of the grave where the body is placed. In other words, while death takes the body, hades is the place where the spirit of a lost man goes. The Lord Jesus spoke of it in that way.

Paul personifies death in Romans 5:14, as he does sin in that same section, and he does it for emphasis. Sin and death entered the world at the same time. Death is the result of sin. During the interval from Adam to Moses, men did not commit the same sin as did Adam, nor was their sinning a transgression of a law, as was Adam's, because the Ten Commandments had not been given. Yet it was a period when men sinned and died. Adam's sin became their sin, for they died as Adam died. Even babies died in the Flood.

Death evidently has an all-inclusive, three-fold meaning that we do not ordinarily attach to it. We think of death as referring only to the body. (1) This is *physical* death, and it refers only to the body. It comes to a man because of Adam's sin. (2) Then there is what is known as *spiritual* death, which is separation from, and rebellion against, God. We inherit a dead nature from Adam; that is, we have no capacity for God and no desire for Him at all. (3) Finally, there is *eternal* death, which is eternal separation from God. Unless a man is redeemed, this inevitably follows. This is the second death that we will find later on in chapter 20, verse 14.

Before Adam sinned, God said to him, ". . . for in the day that thou eatest thereof thou shalt surely die" (Gen. 2:17). Well, Adam lived *physically* for more than nine hundred years after that, but he was dead *spiritually* to God. He ran from God. He no longer had a desire for fellowship with God. He died spiritually, and physical death followed and has come into the human family. More and more it deteriorates mankind. Most of us are being propped up today by modern medicine and the marvelous developments of science in order to stay alive. Actually, the human race is deteriorating all the time. Human life would be much shorter than it is if it were not for all the modern gadgets which keep us alive down here.

Adam is definitely declared here to be a type of Christ. Death must be laid at Adam's door as his total responsibility. You see, God did not create man to die. It was a penalty imposed because Adam transgressed God's command. Because Adam is the federal head of our race, his transgression is our transgression, and his death is our death. Now Christ is the head of a new creation, and this new creation has life only in Christ. He alone can give life. He is totally responsible for the life and eternal bliss of those who are His own.

Dr. Lewis Sperry Chafer put it like this, and this is a theological statement:

> Thus spiritual death comes mediately through an unbroken line of posterity. Over against this, physical death is received from Adam immediately, as each person dies in body because of his own personal share in Adam's first sin.

During the Great Tribulation, death will ride unbridled. The Lord Jesus put it like this: "And except those days should be shortened, there should no flesh be saved: but for the elect's sake those days shall be shortened" (Matt. 24:22).

At the Great White Throne judgment, death will be finally destroyed (see Rev. 20:14). This is confirmed by Paul who writes, "The last enemy that shall be destroyed is death" (1 Cor. 15:26). And John reasserts it in Revelation 21:4: "And God shall wipe away all tears from their eyes; and there shall be no more death, neither sorrow, nor crying, neither shall there be any more pain: for the former things are passed away."

The sword, famine, pestilence, and wild beasts will decimate this earth's population by one-fourth. This is something that, through His prophet Ezekiel, God had said would come: "For thus saith the Lord

GOD; How much more when I send my four sore judgments upon Jerusalem, the sword, and the famine, and the noisome beast, and the pestilence, to cut off from it man and beast?" (Ezek. 14:21).

The pale horse represents plague and pestilence that will stalk the earth. It also encompasses the possibility of germ warfare. Dr. Frank Holtman, head of the University of Tennessee's bacteriological department, said, "While the greater part of a city's population could be destroyed by an atomic bomb, the bacteria method might easily wipe out the entire population within a week."

We have seen the riding of the four horsemen, and this follows exactly the pattern that the Lord Jesus gave while He was on the earth. In Matthew 24:5–8, in the Olivet Discourse, He said: "For many shall come in my name, saying, I am Christ; and shall deceive many [the white horse]. And ye shall hear of wars and rumours of wars [the red horse]: see that ye be not troubled: for all these must come to pass, but the end is not yet. For nation shall rise against nation, and kingdom against kingdom: and there shall be famines [the black horse], and pestilences [the pale horse], and earthquakes, in divers places. All these are the beginning of sorrows." This is the opening of the Great Tribulation.

OPENING OF THE FIFTH SEAL—PRAYER OF THE MARTYRED REMNANT

And when he had opened the fifth seal, I saw under the altar the souls of them that were slain for the word of God, and for the testimony which they held:

And they cried with a loud voice, saying, How long, O Lord, holy and true, dost thou not judge and avenge our blood on them that dwell on the earth? [Rev. 6:9–10].

And when He opened the fifth seal, I saw under the altar of burnt sacrifice the souls [Gr.: psuchas] of those slain on account of the Word of God, and on account of the witness which they had; and they cried with a great voice, saying, How long (until when) O Master, the Holy and True, dost Thou not judge and avenge our blood on them that dwell on the earth (earth dwellers)?

This altar is in heaven and is evidently where Christ offered His blood for the sins of the world. I take the position that His literal blood is in heaven. Let me confirm that with Hebrews 9:23–24 which says: "It was therefore necessary that the patterns of things in the heavens should be purified with these; but the heavenly things themselves with better sacrifices than these. For Christ is not entered into the holy places made with hands, which are the figures of the true; but into heaven itself, now to appear in the presence of God for us."

The souls mentioned here are the Old Testament saints. As the Lord Jesus put it: "That the blood of all the prophets, which was shed from the foundation of the world, may be required of this generation; From the blood of Abel unto the blood of Zacharias, which perished between the altar and the temple: verily I say unto you, It shall be required of this generation" (Luke 11:50–51).

Included with these are those who will be slain in the Great Tribulation Period, as we have already found that one-fourth of the population will be wiped out. They are resting on solid Old Testament ground as they plead for justice on the basis of God's holy law.

And white robes were given unto every one of them; and it was said unto them, that they should rest yet for a little season, until their fellow-servants also and their brethren, that should be killed as they were, should be fulfilled [Rev. 6:11].

My translation of this verse is:

And there was given to them to each one a white robe; and it was said to them, that they should rest (in peace) yet for a little time until their fellow servants also, and their brethren who should be killed even as they were, should be fulfilled.

In other words, the Tribulation saints are to be included with the Old Testament saints in the second resurrection.

OPENING OF THE SIXTH SEAL—THE DAY OF WRATH HAS COME

And I beheld when he had opened the sixth seal, and, lo, there was a great earthquake; and the sun became black as sackcloth of hair, and the moon became as blood;

And the stars of heaven fell unto the earth, even as a fig tree casteth her untimely figs, when she is shaken of a mighty wind [Rev. 6:12–13].

And I saw when He opened the sixth seal, and there was a great earthquake; and the sun became black as sackcloth of hair, and the whole moon became as blood; and the stars of heaven fell into the earth, as a fig tree casteth her unripe figs when she is shaken of a great wind.

This is evidently the beginning of the last half of the Great Tribulation Period. The great day of His wrath is before us. The Great Tribulation opens and closes with these upheavals in the natural universe: (1) The beginning of the Tribulation (compare Joel 2:30–31 with Acts 2:20) and (2) the end of the Tribulation (see Joel 3:9–17; Isa. 13:9–13; 34:1–4; Matt. 24:29.

The fact that we are having an increase in earthquakes today is no fulfillment of this at all. This is to take place in the Great Tribulation Period. But the interesting thing is that in the past earthquakes have really destroyed a great deal of the population of this earth. Professor R. A. Daley, in his book *Our Mobile Earth*, has written this:

> In the last 4,000 years earthquakes have caused the loss of 13,000,000 lives, and by far the most awful earthshock is yet to come. "And there was a great earthquake, such as there was not

since there were men upon the earth, so great an earthquake, so mighty; and the cities of the nations fell" (Rev. 16:18).

What a picture we have here! The earthquakes today are not a fulfillment. They merely show that it could happen as God's Word says it will.

And the heaven departed as a scroll when it is rolled together; and every mountain and island were moved out of their places [Rev. 6:14].

Here is my translation:

And the heaven was removed as a scroll when it is rolled up, and every mountain and island were moved out of their places.

I think that this verse is to be taken quite literally. We see the same thing in Nahum 1:5 and again in chapter 20, verse 11.

And the kings of the earth, and the great men, and the rich men, and the chief captains, and the mighty men, and every bondman, and every free man, hid themselves in the dens and in the rocks of the mountains;

And said to the mountains and rocks, Fall on us, and hide us from the face of him that sitteth on the throne, and from the wrath of the Lamb:

For the great day of his wrath is come; and who shall be able to stand? [Rev. 6:15–17].

And the kings of the earth and the princes, and the chief captains, and the rich, and the strong, and every bondman and free man hid themselves in the caves and rocks of the mountains. And they say to the mountains and to the rocks, Fall on us and hide us from the face of the One sitting on the throne, and from the wrath of the Lamb, for the Great Day of their wrath came, and who is able to stand?

There are those on the earth who are praying to the rocks and to the mountains to fall upon them, because they want to be hidden. Hidden from whom? From the wrath of the Lamb. This is the great day of the wrath of God.

"The wrath of the Lamb" is a paradoxical phrase. The wrath of God is the Day of the Lord, that day that is spoken of all the way through the Old Testament prophets, a day that is coming upon the earth and is yet future. It is called here "the wrath of the Lamb"—that is a strange statement.

The Bible is filled with paradoxes, and I am sure that you have discovered that. A paradox is a proposition which is contrary to received opinion; that is, it is that which is seemingly contradictory. On the surface the assertion seems contradictory, but closer examination reveals it is factual. For example, here are several paradoxes. The farther an object goes from you, the larger it gets. That is not true, but it is true. When a balloon goes up, it gets smaller to the eye, but the balloon is getting larger all the time as the atmosphere gets thinner. Another paradox is that water flows uphill in Sequoia National Park. You may not believe that, but there are tons of water flowing uphill there. The Sequoia National Park is filled with giant redwood trees, and those redwoods are pulling up tons of water all the time. They call it osmosis, which is a scientific word which means they don't really know what is happening. A third paradox is that the closer you get to the sun, the hotter it is. But out in the Hawaiian Islands, a tropical climate, if you look up on the top of Mauna Kea, there is snow up there although it is closer to the sun than you are. May I say to you, there are a lot of paradoxes that are true.

Here we have "the wrath of the Lamb." The lamb is a familiar figure of Christ. Suppose a little lamb, which is noted for gentleness and meekness, did get angry? What then? It is like a tempest in a teapot. From the days of Abel to those of John the Baptist, the Lord Jesus is depicted as a lamb. The apostle John calls Him "the Lamb slain from the foundation of the world" (Rev. 13:8). In other words, God did not choose the lamb because it possessed characteristics of Christ, neither did He choose it for the sacrificial aspect. God *created* such an animal to represent Christ. Christ is the Lamb slain before the foundation of the world, before any lamb was ever created.

The Lord Jesus Christ has the qualities of a lamb. He was meek—"Come unto me, all ye that labour and are heavy laden, and I will give you rest. Take my yoke upon you, and learn of me; for I am meek and lowly in heart: and ye shall find rest unto your souls" (Matt. 11:28–29). He was gentle—". . . Suffer the little children to come unto me, and forbid them not: for of such is the kingdom of God" (Mark 10:14). He was harmless—You never see a sign saying, "Beware of the lamb." You see "Beware of the dog," but not of the lamb. He was humble—Christ washed the feet of His disciples. This is a tremendous thing. He is One whose life was marked by winsomeness. His life was like the perfume of a lovely and fragile flower. His coming was a doxology. His stay was a blessing. His departure was a benediction. Even the unbelieving world has been fascinated by His life. The lamb sets forth His sacrifice. Abraham said, ". . . God will provide himself a lamb . . ." (Gen. 22:8), and God *did* provide Himself a Lamb.

But what about "the wrath"? Wrath is strange and foreign even to the person of God, is it not? God loves the good. God hates the evil. He does not hate as you and I hate. He is not vindictive. God is righteous, God is holy, and He hates that which is contrary to Himself. He says that Jehovah is a man of war. He is strong and mighty. He is mighty in battle. The gospel reveals the wrath of God. Paul said, "For the wrath of God is revealed from heaven against all ungodliness and unrighteousness of men, who hold the truth in unrighteousness" (Rom. 1:18). Look at this world we are in, my friend. It already reveals the wrath of God, the judgment of God.

It is like mixing fire and water to bring wrath and the Lamb together, but all the fury of the wrath of God is revealed in the Lamb. When the Lord Jesus was on earth, He made a scourge of small cords, and He drove the moneychangers out of the temple. Was He bluffing? He was not. He called the religious rulers a generation of vipers, whited sepulchres. He cursed the fig tree. He said, "Woe unto thee, Chorazin and Bethsaida" (see Matt. 11:21). Christ rejected Jerusalem, but He had tears in His eyes when He did so. He still controls the forces of nature, and He uses them in judgment. God has declared war against sin. I say, Blessed be His name. He will not compromise with that which has brought such havoc to the human family! There is a day coming when the wrath of the Lamb will be revealed. Somebody says, "I thought He was gentle and would not punish sin." My friend, God said, "Be wise now therefore, O ye kings: be instructed, ye judges of the earth. Serve the LORD with fear, and rejoice with trembling. Kiss the Son, lest he be angry, and ye perish from the way, when his wrath is kindled but a little. Blessed are all they that put their trust in him" (Ps. 2:10–12).

CHAPTER 7

THEME: *God seals a remnant of Israel and saves a redeemed company of Gentiles*

The Book of Revelation has been labeled a book difficult to understand. Some folk say that it is just a mumbo jumbo of a great many visions which are out of this world and which no one can understand. It is my conviction that this book is very logical and is divided in a very simple manner which no one can miss. If we get bogged down in some passage and try to take symbols and juggle them to fit into any system that we might choose, then we are going to be in real trouble. Rather, we should just let John tell us where we are as we go along. We are now in a section that the Lord Jesus labeled the Great Tribulation. This period takes place after the church leaves the earth, after the church concludes its mission and is taken to be with the Lord. I think that this is not only a reasonable conclusion, but I personally feel it is very clear, not only here, but elsewhere in Scripture.

Peter said that ". . . no prophecy of the scripture is of any private interpretation" (2 Pet. 1:20). In other words, you cannot lift out just one verse here or there or even consider only the Book of Revelation and expect to interpret accurately the whole of prophecy. It is essential to recognize that the Book of Revelation happens to be the last book of the Bible. When you are studying arithmetic in school, you begin with "two plus two equals four." You do not start the little ones in first grade with atomic physics or with higher mathematics. Since this book is the last book of the Bible, the only requirement is to have a working knowledge of the sixty-five books which go before. Then you will find that this book makes a great deal of sense and is quite logical.

John is going into detail now concerning the Great Tribulation Period, a period that has not been elaborated upon in any other place in Scripture except in the Olivet Discourse which the Lord Jesus gave (see Matt. 24–25). John is merely widening that out and giving us additional information. What he says is based on what the Lord Jesus had to say.

In chapter 6 we saw the opening of the seven seals; actually, we have had the opening of only six seals so far. These six seals revealed the four great tragedies that are coming upon the earth, the beginning of the judgments. The fifth seal let us look at a martyred company of people, a great throng. In the sixth seal we were introduced to some of the signs of the doom that is to come upon a godless world in the Great Tribulation Period.

In this period the church is never mentioned by name. The reason it is never mentioned by name is because John is recording things on earth, and at this particular time the church is not on earth. John was told to write the things he had seen, and he saw the vision of the glorified Christ. Then he was to write about "the things which are." He was in the church period, and we are still in it today. Since the church is still in the world, we are in the period of "the things which are." The church was the theme of chapters 2–3: the church in Ephesus, the church in Smyrna, the church in Pergamum, the church in Thyatira, etc. But in the chapter before us there is no talking to the church because the church is not here on earth. We saw in chapters 4–5 that the church was in heaven—that is where the church will go at the time of the Rapture. I will deal later with the reason why the church cannot go through the Great Tribulation Period. There is actually a moral and a theological problem if the church were to enter even one phase of the Tribulation Period.

The subject, therefore, has changed, and we are now talking about things other than the church. We have been introduced to a book with seven seals, and the seals are being removed. Six seals have been removed in the previous chapter. The four horsemen introduce the Great Tribulation Period, and the seven seals give an overall picture of that seven-year period. The last of the seals bears down on the last three and one-half years of the Great Tribulation Period. At this point, one-fourth of the population of the earth has been destroyed in judgment, destroyed in death. I am sure that anyone reading Revelation senses the fact that it is going to be very difficult to make it through this period—especially for those who turn to God, accept Christ, and stand for Him. The question is: Will believers be able to stand for Him during this period?

John is now going to put down another principle which he will follow because he knows that you and I are going to have trouble with the Revelation. Therefore he has made it very simple for us. He introduces series of sevens, but the way that he deals with them is the important thing for us to see. A format is followed from the breaking of the seals to the bowls of wrath. Between the sixth and seventh of each, there is an interlude of seemingly extraneous matter, but it is explanatory matter—it explains the action and answers certain questions. This is what chapter 7 will do for us. This principle of an explanatory interval will be true of the seven trumpets, of the seven performers and of the seven bowls of wrath. You will find John following this principle all the way through this particular section of Revelation, so that we do not lose our way.

We need now to deal with the question that any reasonable person would raise at this point: What about people turning to God and getting saved during this period? Second Thessalonians makes it clear that the Holy Spirit, the Restrainer, is removed from the earth (see 2 Thess. 2:7). He has taken the church to present it to Christ. Since you cannot have any turning to God without the work of the Holy Spirit, will anybody get saved without the Holy Spirit being present on the earth?

My friend, the Holy Spirit will be present. I did not say that the Holy Spirit will have left the world but that He no longer will restrain evil. The Holy Spirit came on the Day of Pentecost to perform a specific ministry of calling out a body of believers in the church which is referred to as the body of Christ. When the church is removed from the earth, that peculiar ministry of the Holy Spirit will end. One of His ministries in this particular era has been that of restraining evil. It was absolutely essential that He be a restrainer in order for the gospel to penetrate a Satan-controlled and Satan-blinded world. How could the Word go out unless the Spirit of God held back evil? Just think of the forces of evil that are working against the getting out of the Word of God today. In my own experience with our Bible-teaching radio ministry, we just sailed along like a breeze for a year or two. Then problems came along. I became ill, and all sorts of things took place. When we finally regained our equilibrium and began to look around, we saw what was happening: the enemy was busy. Believe me, if the Restrainer had not been at work, I am sure that we would have been removed from the scene.

How are people going to get saved during the period of the Great Tribulation if the Holy Spirit will not be restraining evil? The Great Tribulation is the Devil's holiday. That is the day when he is going to have freedom to do as he pleases. We will see why God is going to grant that: it is a period of the judgment of God upon a Christ-rejecting world. Then, does anybody get saved in the Great Tribulation period? My friend, I believe that there will be a greater company saved in that period than in any other seven-year period in the history of the world. Chapter 7 is going to tell us how that will take place. The Holy Spirit is in the world after the church is removed just as He was in the world before Pentecost. In reading the Old Testament, you will find the Spirit of God working in the hearts and lives of men and women. Many multitudes were brought to God, but He was not restraining evil in the world, and He was not baptizing believers into the body of the church in the Old Testament. That is what He is doing today, but that ministry will cease. However, He will still be in the business of getting men and women to Christ. He will continue His ministry which has always been one of taking God's creation and renovating it. We are told in the beginning, ". . . the spirit of God moved [brooded] upon the face of the waters" (Gen. 1:2). The Spirit of God broods over this earth today and has from the very beginning and will continue doing so after the church is removed from the earth. He will have to have an unusual, special program during this period, and John is now going to tell us what that program is going to be.

REASON FOR THE INTERLUDE

The reason for the interlude between the sixth and seventh seals is given to us in the first three verses of this chapter.

And after these things I saw four angels standing on the four corners of the earth, holding the four winds of the earth, that the wind should not blow on the earth, nor on the sea, nor on any tree [Rev. 7:1].

I give my own translation simply in an attempt to give the literal words and try to say what John was saying:

> *After this I saw four angels standing on the four corners of the earth, holding firmly the four winds of the earth, that no wind might blow on the earth nor on the sea, nor on any tree.*

"After this" refers to the tremendous judgment of the previous chapter, the riding of the four horsemen. In the riding of the four horsemen I believe we have been given a bird's-eye view of the Great Tribulation Period, an overall picture, and now the details are going to be given to us.

"After this I saw four angels standing on the four corners of the earth." A smart-alecky young fellow got up at a meeting years ago where Dr. Harry Ironside was speaking and said: "I told you the Bible was unscientific! The Bible teaches that the earth is flat because it says 'the four corners of the earth.'" Dr. Ironside replied, "Young man, I am amazed that you didn't know that the earth has four corners. They are North, East, South, and West." Those are the four corners, and that is the direction of the four angels. There is one in the North, the East, the South, and the West.

"Holding firmly the four winds of the earth, that no wind might blow on the earth, nor on the sea, nor on any tree." These would be the winds of judgment. God uses wind in judgment, and He controls the wind. Psalm 148:8 says, "Fire, and hail; snow, and vapours; stormy wind fulfilling his word."

The winds of judgment are now to be held back. Nothing can move until God accomplishes His purpose. What is His purpose going to be? I do not think God would permit any period to continue on this earth in which there were not some of the human family turning to God, because that is His purpose. I do not think He would continue to keep this world running; I think He would shut it down, turn it off, and speak it out of existence if there were not folk turning to Him. Therefore, this will be a period when multitudes will turn to Him.

A great company is going to be saved, and this reveals that these judgments will accomplish a purpose for God. It will cause multitudes to turn to Him in this period, and it will cause another multitude to turn against Him. It is just like the effect of the sun shining down on a piece of soft clay. What will the sun do to the clay? It will harden it. What would be the effect of that same sunlight upon wax? It would melt it. The sun has the opposite effect upon clay and wax. The judgments of God are the same. In our lives as believers, when trouble comes to us—I've discovered this in my own life—it will either draw us to God or drive us from Him. We need to be drawn to Him, and that is the reason the Lord lets some of us have sicknesses. He wants to draw us closer to Himself, and this is His way of doing it.

We cannot explain every little detail here in this chapter—at least, *I* cannot. I get a little irritated and provoked that I do not know as much as some of these so-called prophetic teachers claim to know today. They seem to have a private line in to the Lord. They now know the date when the Lord is coming again, and not only that, they can actually interpret some of these passages in the most amazing fashion. Where the Scriptures say that the blood during the War of Armageddon will be up to the bridle bits, some of these fellows can tell you the type of blood it is! They irritate me because I don't seem to be able to get that kind of information—and then I wonder what the value of it is when you get it. To begin with, the church ought to understand clearly that we have been delivered from going through this period. The Lord Jesus said, "Verily, verily, I say unto you, He that heareth my word, and believeth on him that sent me, hath [right now] everlasting [eternal] life, and shall not come into condemnation [judgment]; but is passed from death unto life" (John 5:24). The Great Tribulation is a judgment, and the church is not coming into it. He made it clear to the church of Philadelphia that He was going to deliver them from that hour. What hour? The hour that John is talking about right now. We need to let Scripture speak for itself.

> **And I saw another angel ascending from the east, having the seal of the living God: and he cried with a loud voice to the four angels, to whom it was given to hurt the earth and the sea,**
>
> **Saying, Hurt not the earth, neither the sea, nor the trees, till we have sealed the servants of our God in their foreheads [Rev. 7:2–3].**

Again, this is my translation:

> *And I saw another angel ascending from (the) sunrising, having (the) seal of (the) Living God, and he cried with a great voice to the four angels, to whom it had been given to hurt the earth and the sea, saying, Hurt not the earth, nor the sea, nor the trees, until we shall have sealed the servants (bond slaves) of our God, in their foreheads.*

"Another angel" means this is a fifth angel. He is apparently of a higher rank than the other four because he gives them orders. As we see in the Book of Daniel and also in the Epistle to the Ephesians, there are gradations of orders of angels, both good and bad. Satan has the demon world well organized; he probably has generals, lieutenant colonels, majors, lieutenants, sergeants, and then a great many privates. On the other side, God also has His angels arranged. This angel gives orders to the other four.

"He cried with a great voice." In the Greek this is *phōne megale*. If you turn *phōne megale* around, you can see where we get our English word *megaphone*. Megale means "great"; *phōne* means "noise or voice."

This is an indication that frightful and fearful judgment is getting ready to break upon the earth, and it is therefore necessary to secure the servants of God. If He does not seal them, they are not going to make it through. However, they are going to be preserved in this day of wrath that is coming on the earth. The Lord Jesus Himself mentioned this in Matthew 24:21–22: "For then shall be great tribulation, such as was not since the beginning of the world to this time, no, nor ever shall be. And except those days should be shortened, there should no flesh be saved: but for the elect's sake those days shall be shortened." For the sake of these who have been sealed, this terrible time will be shortened.

What is the mark that is put upon their foreheads? Now here is a place where I must confess (I sure hope you won't let this get out) that I do not know the answer, and I can only make suggestions. There are many who know what the mark is, but the interesting thing is that you cannot get any two of them to agree as to what it is. I have come to the conclusion that they are all wrong. We are not told what it is, and I do not think it is important for the church to know what the mark is. We are simply told that they are going to be marked. We do know that there are those who will not be able to trade during this period when the Antichrist comes to power unless they have the mark of the Beast. This mark of God's is in contrast to the mark of the Beast. My feeling is that it is a spiritual mark that will be in their lives: ". . . by their fruits ye shall know them" (Matt. 7:20)—by their lives. I believe that is going to be the mark of God's own during this period because the godless are really going to be godless in this period. I personally don't see how they can be any more godless than the godless in the world today, but the Word of God says they can go much farther than they have gone even in our day.

We now have this interlude before the seventh seal is opened. This angel is apparently more than a sergeant; he is probably a lieutenant colonel or a general. He says, "Hold everything! Hold back the winds of judgment, the winds of the Great Tribulation Period, because we have to seal these folk so they can make it through." There will be two great companies sealed, one out of the nation Israel and the other out of the Gentiles.

Where is the church? The church is not here; they are with Christ in, I believe, the New Jerusalem. He said that He was going to prepare a place for those who were His, and now that He has taken them off the earth, they are with Him. That city will come down from God a little later on in the Revelation, and we will get a look at it.

The reason, therefore, for the interlude between the sixth and seventh seals is to make sure that these sealed ones are going to make it through the Great Tribulation Period. The Lord Jesus made it very clear that they *are* going to make it through.

REMNANT OF ISRAEL SEALED

When God deals with Israel, I have always noticed that He deals with dates and He deals with numbers. When He is dealing with the church, He does not deal with either dates or numbers. Paul never turned in a report to anybody as to how many were saved. Even when we get to the great company of Gentiles who are saved in the Great Tribulation Period, the number is not given. When God deals with Israel, however, He deals with numbers and He deals with dates. The insistence of some Bible teachers to set dates for these prophetic events has hurt the study of prophecy and has brought it down to a low level, whereas this aspect ought to be kept on as high a level as any other subject of prophecy.

> **And I heard the number of them which were sealed: and there were sealed an hundred and forty and four thousand of all the tribes of the children of Israel [Rev. 7:4].**
>
> *And I heard the number of those sealed, a hundred and forty and four thousand, sealed out of every tribe of the children of Israel.*

One hundred forty-four thousand is the number sealed from the nation Israel, but we will see that out of the earth there will be a multitude of Gentiles saved—too numerous to count. I notice that all the evangelists and preachers today are able to give you a count of the number saved in their meetings. In fact, some may give you a count that is a little bit larger than it really is. But here is one company of saved that they couldn't count.

Apparently, in the Great Tribulation there is going to be a great company who are to be saved. How are they going to be saved? They are going to be sealed. The Holy Spirit is going to be here, not only to regenerate them, but He will also have a special ministry of sealing in this period. The seal guarantees that they are going to be delivered. When you go down to the post office to register a letter, a postal clerk puts a stamp on it and puts a seal on it, and you pay a little extra for that. That seal means that the entire postal department is going to get behind that letter and see that it is delivered. They may be a little late in delivering it, but they guarantee that they are going to deliver it. That is what "sealed" means here. The Holy Spirit guarantees that they will make it through the Great Tribulation. If it weren't for the seal, they wouldn't make it through.

If you really want to know the truth, Vernon McGee would not make it through today if it weren't for the Holy Spirit. I wonder if you and I really realize how weak we are? I would deny Him before the sun went down if it wasn't for His work in me by the Spirit of God. We all have that nature which is in rebellion against God.

This company of the 144,000 can be identified without any speculation whatsoever. To me it is almost nonsense for any group to claim that they are the 144,000. Two cults did that in their beginnings, but then they passed 144,000 in membership. Apparently, they were not very optimistic when they started out. They say they take it literally, but they have a problem, now that they have passed that number. They should have gone out of business when they got to 144,000, but they didn't.

This number does not refer to any group in existence today, nor does it refer to the church. During the Great Tribulation, 144,000 are going to be saved "out of every tribe of the children of *Israel.*" If you think that you are in the 144,000, you are not only saying that you belong to Israel, but you also had better know your tribe because the tribes are going to be identified.

It is very clear that God will have a remnant of His people who are going to be saved. This may seem to you like a big number, but actually, it is very small. There are over fourteen million Jews today in the world, and in comparison to that number, you can see that the remnant of the children of Israel is really going to be very small.

There is no use speculating here or trying to draw on symbols. Some even say that the number—144,000—is a symbol of another number. Cannot God say what He wants to say? Cannot He count? Certainly He can. If He says 144,000, I do not think He means 145,000. I think He means exactly 144,000.

"Out of every tribe of the children of Israel." From the day God called Abraham, there has always been a remnant that is true to God. There is a remnant today. I know many wonderful Christian Jews. I don't know why I say "Christian Jews" since I don't say Christian Americans or Christian Germans. But we do say this of Israel because of the fact that there is the remnant that trusts Christ in our day. It is not a large remnant, but there is not a very large remnant of Gentiles either. I suppose that the great minority group is that of real believers in Christ.

Paul says in Romans 9:8: "That is, They which are the children of the flesh, these are not the children of God: but the children of the promise are counted for the seed."

That is true today. Again Paul writes in Romans 11:4–5: "But what saith the answer of God unto him? I have reserved to myself seven thousand men, who have not bowed the knee to the image of Baal. Even so then at this present time also there is a remnant according to the election of grace." Paul said that in his day there was a remnant in the church. There is a remnant in our day in the church. During the Great Tribulation there will be a remnant, and the number is 144,000.

These are the ones who are going to witness of Christ in the Great Tribulation Period. In Matthew 24:14, speaking of this period, the Lord Jesus said: "And this gospel of the kingdom shall be preached in all the world for a witness unto all nations; and then shall the end come."

Some will say that the gospel of the kingdom is a different gospel. Of course, it is not. God has never had but one way to save sinners, and that is through the death of Christ. If you had asked Abel when he brought that little lamb to God, "Abel, do you think that little lamb will save you?" he would have said, "No, this little lamb is representing the One who God told my mother was coming from a woman to be the Savior of the world. This little lamb typifies Him." John the Baptist almost stepped out of character when he said, ". . . Behold the Lamb of God, which taketh away the sin of the world" (John 1:29). The gospel of the kingdom is the gospel of the death and burial and resurrection of Christ, which is going to alert the nation Israel, and many will turn to Christ. These will preach the gospel, but they will have something to add that we have no right to say today. They will say, "And then shall the end come." In other words, it is not going to be long until He will be back. We have no right to say that Christ will be returning soon, because we know neither the day nor the hour when He shall come.

> **Of the tribe of Juda were sealed twelve thousand. Of the tribe of Reuben were sealed twelve thousand. Of the tribe of Gad were sealed twelve thousand.**
>
> **Of the tribe of Aser were sealed twelve thousand. Of the tribe of Nepthalim were sealed twelve thousand. Of the tribe of Manasses were sealed twelve thousand.**
>
> **Of the tribe of Simeon were sealed twelve thousand. Of the tribe of Levi were sealed twelve thousand. Of the tribe of Issachar were sealed twelve thousand.**
>
> **Of the tribe of Zabulon were sealed twelve thousand. Of the tribe of Joseph were sealed twelve thousand. Of the tribe of Benjamin were sealed twelve thousand [Rev. 7:5–8].**

Here is my translation:

> *Of the tribe of Judah were sealed twelve thousand; of the tribe of Reuben twelve thousand; of the tribe of Gad twelve thousand, of the tribe of Asher twelve thousand; of the tribe of Naphtali twelve thousand; of the tribe of*

Manasseh twelve thousand; of the tribe of Simeon twelve thousand; of the tribe of Levi twelve thousand; of the tribe of Issachar twelve thousand; of the tribe of Zebulun twelve thousand; of the tribe of Joseph twelve thousand; of the tribe of Benjamin were sealed twelve thousand.

Twelve thousand are sealed out of each tribe. The 144,000 are divided by twelve, and one-twelfth is in each tribe, so that we know that John is talking about the children of Israel. I do not see how anyone can spiritualize this and attempt to appropriate it either to themselves or to some group other than the children of Israel. God promised, as we see again and again in the Old Testament, that He would come and establish His kingdom, which we will see is first a thousand-year kingdom, a time of testing, and then moves right into eternity.

We are given here the twelve tribes of Israel. One writer says that there are thirteen times in the Bible that the twelve tribes are listed, and another writer says that they are given eighteen times. I do not know which is accurate, but in every case where the twelve tribes are named, it is always *twelve* tribes. Sometimes changes are made, and I cannot always determine the reason for the changes, but I know that God had something in mind when He did it.

There are certain peculiarities in this list which I will call to your attention, but I don't think it is essential to go into detail concerning these twelve tribes. First of all, you will notice that Judah heads the list. The tribe of Reuben should come first, for Reuben was the oldest, but because of his very gross immorality, he lost the first place—but he is still included. The question often arises: When a Christian sins, does he lose his salvation? No, but he may lose his reward. Very frankly, there will be many Christians who are saved but who indulged in sin and will lose their reward. Reuben is a very good example of how God deals, and this principle is set down here. Reuben lost first place, he lost the place of honor, but he did not lose out altogether. He is mentioned here, but he is number two; he should have been number one. Judah was the tribe given preeminence (see Gen. 49:8–10) and was the tribe from which the Lord Jesus came.

We also find that the tribes of Dan and Ephraim are omitted from this list. Both of these tribes were guilty of leading the nation into idolatry.

In history you will find that Dan was the first tribe that fell into idolatry (see Jud. 18:30). The tribe of Dan later on became the headquarters for calf worship whereby "Jeroboam made Israel to sin" (see 1 Kings 12:28–30). That Dan is given top priority in the Millennium (see Ezek. 48) reveals that the grace of God can reach down and meet the needs of any sinner. The tribe of Dan is in the Millennium, but they are not sealed for the purpose of witnessing during the time of the Great Tribulation. I think that this tribe lost out a great deal.

Ephraim was also guilty of idolatry. In Hosea 4:17 we read, "Ephraim is joined to idols: let him alone." That has reference to the entire northern kingdom of Israel, but remember that Ephraim was the leader there. Also, Ephraim was the tribe which led in the division of the kingdom (see 1 Kings 11:26).

In the list of the 144,000 who will be sealed, Joseph takes the place of Ephraim, and to take the place of Dan is Levi. Levi was the priestly tribe, and they are going to be witnesses in the Great Tribulation Period, which is quite proper.

I trust that we can understand and see that God has now turned again to the nation of Israel. He has not given them up. He said, "How shall I give thee up, Ephraim? . . ." (Hos. 11:8). In other words God said, "I can't do it," and God didn't give them up. They are going to make it through the Great Tribulation Period even though they will lose out as witness for God during that period.

The Old Testament is filled with prophecy that God has given to these people that they are to be a nation forever and that they are to be in the land of Israel forever. If you come to the New Testament and write Israel off as having disappeared and that God is through with them, you have to contradict the whole tenor and tone of the Old Testament. I have said that the Book of Revelation is like a great union station or an airport where trains or planes come in from everywhere: all the major themes of prophecy come in to Revelation. Therefore, you would certainly expect Israel to be here in the Book of Revelation—and, lo and behold, here it is.

"Israel" means Israel. If God had wanted to call Israel the church, I think He would have just said "church" because He was able to say "church" when the time came. But now the church is not mentioned anymore, and He is talking about Israel and the 144,000 who are sealed to witness for Him.

The 144,000 are sealed, especially because they are going to witness during this period, and it is going to cost them a great deal. If they were not sealed, they sure wouldn't be able to make it through. God never leaves Himself without a witness upon this earth.

REDEEMED MULTITUDE OF GENTILES

After this I beheld, and lo, a great multitude, which no man could number, of all nations, and kindreds, and people, and tongues, stood before the throne, and before the Lamb, clothed with white robes, and palms in their hands;

And cried with a loud voice, saying, Salvation to our God which sitteth upon the throne, and unto the Lamb [Rev. 7:9–10].

After these things I saw, and behold, a great multitude which no man could number, out of every nation and out of tribes, and peoples, and tongues, standing before the throne and before the Lamb arrayed (clothed) in white robes and palm branches in their hands; and they cry with a great voice saying, The salvation to our God, who sitteth on the throne and to the Lamb.

"After these things I saw." John is seeing as well as hearing these things.

"And behold, a great multitude which no man could number." Someone will say, "You mean to tell me that men couldn't count that crowd?" What it says is that no *one* man could number these—and it doesn't say anything about a computer. It says that no one man could number this crowd because it is such a large crowd. I wouldn't dare to venture any guess whatsoever, but the size of this multitude is obviously stupendous. It is not a one-man job to number them.

"Out of every nation and out of tribes, and peoples, and tongues." These are Gentiles, people from every tribe and nation under the sun. This means that in the Great Tribulation the gospel of the kingdom will be preached through the world. I want to repeat this: the 144,000 witnesses in the Great Tribulation Period are going to do in seven years what the church up to the present has not done in over nineteen hundred years. Do not boast about your missionary program. None of us are reaching very many. But, during the Great Tribulation, there will be a great company of people who will be saved.

It is my own judgment—I don't think that Scripture says this anywhere, because nothing has yet to be fulfilled before the Lord removes the church—but it looks to me now as if He is going to let the world hear the gospel before the Rapture of the church. I believe that radio is one of the media that will be used. I think there are other media that will be used: the tape ministry, the printed page, and evangelism. Many evangelists are reaching multitudes of people today. Other radio programs are doing a much bigger job than we are doing, but if you put us all together, we are making quite an impact on this world in which we live.

"Standing before the throne and before the Lamb." Here is a great company who have come out of the Great Tribulation Period and are rejoicing in their salvation. They are redeemed and have made it through the Great Tribulation Period. Again may I say, the greatest days of God's salvation are in the future.

It is possible that most of this company were martyred during the Great Tribulation Period, but they were faithful to the end. The Lord Jesus said in the Olivet Discourse, speaking of this same period, "But he that shall endure unto the end, the same shall be saved" (Matt. 24:13). Did they endure to the end because they gritted their teeth, clenched their fists, and pulled themselves up by their bootstraps? No, they didn't do that at all—they were sealed by the Holy Spirit.

The "white robes" set before us the righteousness of Christ in which they are clothed. We cannot stand before God in our own righteousness because our own righteousness is as filthy rags, and I do not think you are going to wear filthy rags in the presence of God.

"Palm branches" is literally in the Greek "palm trees." They are the sign of victory, victory in Christ. This multitude is part of the great triumphal entry that will occur when Christ returns to the earth. The triumphal entry has really never taken place yet. That was actually more like a triumphal exit when He rode into Jerusalem on that little donkey, for He was getting ready to leave the earth, and He was on the way to the cross at that time. Since then, there has been a great company who have come to Him, and in the Great Tribulation there will be another great company. When He returns to the earth, the great company, martyred for Him in the Great Tribulation, will be included in the first resurrection, and they are going to be there. This is a wonderful, glorious picture that is given to us.

And all the angels stood round about the throne, and about the elders and the four beasts, and fell before the throne on their faces, and worshipped God,

Saying, Amen: Blessing, and glory, and wisdom, and thanksgiving, and honour, and power, and might, be unto our God for ever and ever. Amen [Rev. 7:11–12].

And all the angels were standing around the throne, and about the elders and the four living creatures; and they fell before the throne on their faces, and worshipped God, saying, Amen, blessing, and glory, and wisdom, and thanksgiving, and honor, and power, and might, be unto your God for ever and ever. Amen.

This is a fabulous, fantastic scene of universal worship of God by His creatures. The church is here, the Old Testament saints are here, and the Tribulation saints are here. And now the angels join in on it.

There are just one or two things I would like to say about the angels. I do not want to labor the point, and I would not contend with anyone about it, but nowhere in Scripture does it say that angels sing. They are *saying* this here. However, the important thing to note is that the other companies thank God for their redemption, "Salvation to our God," but the angels do not mention it. They praise God for His attributes and goodness, but not for salvation. Why? They are sinless creatures, not redeemed sinners. I do not think the angels will be able to sing, but I do believe that Vernon McGee will be able to sing in that day. I cannot do it now, but I sure will be able to sing with that great company.

I hope that this will begin to broaden your vision and your comprehension as to what heaven is going to be. A great many people think that the only ones to be in heaven are their little group, their little church, or their little denomination. Well, my friend, there will be other redeemed people there besides even the church. I think that it will surprise a lot of the saints to discover this when they get to heaven. I wish that we could discover it down here because it would give us a greater love for God and lead us to worship Him more in a very real way, to worship Him in spirit and truth.

One of the elders now wants to bring John up to date on what is taking place:

> **And one of the elders answered, saying unto me, What are these which are arrayed in white robes? and whence came they?**
>
> **And I said unto him, Sir, thou knowest. And he said to me, These are they which came out of great tribulation, and have washed their robes, and made them white in the blood of the Lamb [Rev. 7:13–14].**
>
> *And one of the elders answered, saying unto me, These which are arrayed in the white robes, who are they, and whence came they? And I say unto him, My lord, thou knowest. And he said to me, These are they which came out of the great tribulation, and they washed their robes, and made them white in the blood of the Lamb.*

This is a very enlightening passage of Scripture. One of the elders went over to John and said, "John, who are these believers here arrayed in the white robes?" And John said, "My lord, thou knowest." This is an idiomatic expression, and I think we have one like it in our day. When someone asks us a question and we don't know the answer, we just sort of lift up our hands and say, "Search me!" which means, "I don't know!" This is exactly what John is saying here: "You know that I don't know. You tell me because I don't know."

"And he said to me, These are they which came out of great tribulation." If these people gathered here were the church, John would have known it. John wrote to the believers in his day. He knew about the church, he knew about the body of believers, and he wrote to them about love, that great unifying cement that holds them together. But John doesn't know who this company is. The elder, who is a representative of the church now in heaven, knows that this company is not the church. It is an altogether different company. It is those who came out of *the* Great Tribulation. Doesn't that tell you that the church is not going through the Great Tribulation? This is a special company, out of all tribes and tongues and nations, who have come out of the Great Tribulation.

We live in a day when God makes a division in the human family. One division is between the saved and the lost, of course—that is the great bifurcation of the human family. But if you want a racial division or a group division of the human family, the Word of God has something to say about it: "Give none offence, neither to the Jews, nor to the Gentiles, nor to the church of God" (1 Cor. 10:32). Paul says to the Corinthians that there are three groups—the Jews, the Gentiles, and the church of God—and they are not to give offense to any one of these groups. This is one of the divisions that the Scripture makes of the human family. The Jews, Gentiles, and the church of God comprise the division that runs right down through the human family today. In the Great Tribulation, we come to a period when there are but two groups: Jews and Gentiles. Where is the church of God? It went to be with Him. The Lord Jesus said, ". . . I go to prepare a place for you. And if I go and prepare a place for you, I will come again, and receive you unto myself . . ." (John 14:2–3). The church is with Him in heaven as we move through the Revelation. In 1 Corinthians 12:13 Paul says: "For by one Spirit we are all baptized into one body, whether we be

Jews or Gentiles, whether we be bond or free; and have been all made to drink into one Spirit." God today is calling out of the two divisions, both Jews and Gentiles, a people for His name that are different—the church—and that church will be taken out of the world.

I do not like the impression given today by some—it is a pessimistic viewpoint—that somehow or another God is failing. My friend, God is doing exactly what He said He was going to do: that in this age He would call a people out of this world to Himself. He is doing a much better job at that than you and I think He is. When I was a pastor of a church, I did not think He was doing very much, but I have discovered as our radio ministry has reached out across this land and around the world that there are multitudes who are turning to Christ everywhere. And others are reporting the same thing. God is calling a people out of this world to Himself.

John makes it clear that this group he sees in heaven is different from the church. They came through *the* Great Tribulation. Let me remind you that it was the Lord Jesus Christ Himself who gave us the term, "great tribulation." Some may think that some rank, wildhaired fundamentalist thought of this term, but the Lord Jesus Christ is the One who thought of it and designated this period as the Great Tribulation. In Matthew 24:21 He says: "For then shall be great tribulation, such as was not since the beginning of the world to this time, no, nor ever shall be." Both in Matthew and in Revelation, it is expressed in the Greek in a way we cannot express in English. There is an article with the adjective *great* and an article with *tribulation;* it is "the tribulation, the great one." It is given to us like that for emphasis. In other words, this is something that is different; this is something that is indeed unique.

Let me repeat that when John is quizzed by one of the elders, he is unable to identify this great company. John would have known them if this were the church; or if they were Old Testament saints or Israelites, I think John would have known it. This company he does not recognize at all. They are identified as redeemed Gentiles who have come out of the Great Tribulation.

Their robes were white, which speaks of the righteousness of

Christ. How did they get that righteousness? It is because Christ shed His blood. The only reason that you and I will be able to stand before God is because Christ paid the penalty for our sins. He died that you and I might live, and that is true of this group here also. It has always been true that God has only one way of saving mankind, and it is by faith in the death and resurrection of Jesus Christ. Paul wrote: "Moreover, brethren, I declare unto you the gospel which I preached unto you, which also ye have received, and wherein ye stand; By which also ye are saved, if ye keep in memory what I preached unto you, unless ye have believed in vain. For I delivered unto you first of all that which I also received, how that Christ died for our sins according to the scriptures; And that he was buried, and that he rose again the third day according to the scriptures" (1 Cor. 15:1–4). "For I delivered unto you first of all that which I also received." Paul says that this is not new with him. He did not originate it. It was given to him when the Lord Jesus taught him for two years out yonder in the Arabian desert.

Now this is the gospel: "How that Christ died for our sins according to the scriptures [according to the Old Testament]; And that he was buried, and that he rose again the third day according to the scriptures." The gospel is not God asking you to do something; it is God telling you that He has done something for you. The gospel is not your giving something to God; the gospel is God's giving something to you. The gift of God is eternal life in Christ Jesus. How do you get it? By faith. That is the only way you can receive a gift. Suppose it is Christmastime and you come to me and say, "Dr. McGee, here is a gift for you." Now what do I have to do to receive it? I could say to you, "I'll come and mow your lawn for you." But you would say, "I don't want you to mow my lawn. This is a *gift*." I would insult you if I tried to pay you for your gift. Suppose I offered you the few cents in my pocket in exchange for your gift—that would be an insult. My friend, the thing has gotten all mixed up today. The gospel is what God has done for us. It is His gift.

Again Paul writes in Ephesians 1:7: "In whom we have redemption through his blood, the forgiveness of sins, according to the riches of his grace." God has plenty of grace. It does not matter who you are, He can save you. You may think you are a dirty, mean sinner. Well, that is the only kind He saves—we are all that.

We have therefore this great company of Gentiles who are not part of the church. We need to enlarge our conception of the redeemed to the extent that it goes beyond the borders of the church and certainly beyond the borders of your little group or denomination or my little group.

Therefore are they before the throne of God, and serve him day and night in his temple: and he that sitteth on the throne shall dwell among them.

They shall hunger no more, neither thirst any more; neither shall the sun light on them, nor any heat.

For the Lamb which is in the midst of the throne shall feed them, and shall lead them unto living fountains of waters: and God shall wipe away all tears from their eyes [Rev. 7:15–17].

Therefore are they before the throne of God, and serve Him day and night in His temple (sanctuary); and He that sitteth on the throne shall spread His tabernacle (tent) over them. They shall hunger no more, neither thirst any more; neither shall the sun strike upon them, nor any heat (scorching wind): for the Lamb in the midst of the throne shall be their shepherd, and shall guide them into fountains of waters of life; and God shall wipe away every tear from their eyes.

"Therefore are they before the throne of God, and serve him day and night in his temple." We now know for sure that this is not the church, for the church is never identified with the temple. At the end of this book, when the church is in the New Jerusalem, there is no temple there. The church will never have a temple. There is going to be one here on the earth, but there is not one in heaven where the church is. Therefore, this could not be the church.

"And He that sitteth on the throne shall spread His tabernacle (tent) over them." This is for their protection, you see.

This company has had it; they have been through the Great Tribulation. Most of them, I believe, were martyrs and laid down their lives for Christ. Although we are not specifically told that, they are presented to us as being before the throne of God in heaven. The things that are mentioned now are things they have endured. They are not going to hunger or thirst—they apparently did. They have been out in the burning heat of the sun. They have also been thirsty for spiritual things which they did not have. And they wept, but now God will wipe away every tear from their eyes. They made it through the Great Tribulation because of the blood of the Lamb. This is a wonderful company of folk that is presented to us here.

My friend, the Lord Jesus has other sheep. He told His disciples, and it was hard for them to understand: "And other sheep I have, which are not of this fold . . ." (John 10:16). He could say the same thing to the church today, "I have other sheep that you do not know anything about." This company of Gentiles are some of the other sheep who will be redeemed but are not a part of the church.

CHAPTER 8

THEME: *Opening the seventh seal*

In chapter 8 we have the opening of the seventh seal which introduces the seven angels blowing seven trumpets. Four of the trumpets will be dealt with in this chapter. After the parenthetical matter of chapter 7, the sealing to two companies, we now have the opening of the seals resumed. Only the seventh seal remains to be opened. This is the pattern that John sets for the remainder of the Book of Revelation so that we cannot be led astray. There will be series of sevens and, in fact, there are four such series which relate to the Great Tribulation Period. John will give the first six of whatever the series is. Then he will present parenthetical material that contributes to the understanding of that particular series. Finally, the opening of the seventh of the series will introduce the next series of seven, which means that these series are interrelated, tied together, and actually belong to the same period.

There is no reason to get bogged down or to be sensational at this point. To begin with, we have said that everything from chapter 4 on is future—"the things that shall be after these things" (see Rev. 1:19). We are living in the things that are present, the church age, and in one sense these things do not concern us. Many people say, "Oh, it frightens me to study the Book of Revelation!" I will admit that, beginning with the riding of the four horsemen of the Apocalypse, these are terrible, terrific judgments that are coming on this earth. They are so tremendous that they boggle the mind just to read about them. But we can at least know where we are: these are things that will take place after the church has left the earth. If you are a child of God, you have been sealed by the Holy Spirit to be delivered to Christ when the church goes out of the world before the Great Tribulation Period. This is what is called "the blessed hope" of the church.

These seven trumpets will bring us to the full intensity of the Great Tribulation. The seven seals bring judgments which are the natural results of the activities of sinful man apart from God. The sixth seal brings the judgment of nature. The seven trumpets reveal that God is directly and supernaturally judging a rebellious race.

The seven seals, the seven trumpets, the seven personalities, and the seven vials or bowls of wrath all concern the same period, but from a little different angle. (1) In the seven seals we see the judgment which is the result of man's willful activity. The judgment of God will be coming upon sinful man. In the first seal we saw the riding of the white horse—a false peace; "For when they shall say, Peace and safety; then sudden destruction cometh upon them . . ." (1 Thess. 5:3). The second seal was the riding of the red horse of war. War comes because it is in the heart of man. A great many people think that if we took all the guns away from people, if there were no arms and no atom bombs, then we would have peace on the earth. My friend, war is in the heart of man, and you have to change the heart of man before you can get rid of war. Frankly, I would have more confidence in a real, born-again Christian who has a gun than an unsaved man who does not have a gun, because if he is unarmed, he can still choke his victim to death. We are seeing that murder is in the human heart. (2) In the seven trumpets, to which we are coming in this chapter, we see the judgment which is the direct activity of God. (3) When we come to the seven personalities, we will see the judgment which is the result of Satan's fight against God. Satan will be brought out in the open at that time. (4) In the seven bowls of wrath, we will see the final judgment of the Great Tribulation, which is the direct activity of God because of man's and Satan's rebellion—God will judge both, by the way.

As we come to this section in which symbols will be used, let us remember that a symbol is a symbol of a fact. We will find that there is a strange and strong similarity between the plagues of Egypt in Moses' day and the trumpet judgments. It is quite reasonable and logical to conclude hat if the plagues of Moses were literal, then the plagues that are coming in the Great Tribulation Period are going to be literal. The symbols that are used are symbols of the reality which is coming. Plain language could not make it clear to our minds how terrible and tragic the Great Tribulation will be. It beggars description, and so God exhausts language and brings in symbols. It is well to keep in mind that this book is a revelation of Jesus Christ. We see Him now in a new role of Judge. The symbols that are used are not hazy and shadowy symbols which can be dissipated into thin air by some specious system of hermeneutics. When symbols are used—and they are used in this book—the key to their meaning is supplied. Scripture will furnish the explanation, and you do not need to draw upon your imagination.

The Book of Revelation is the last book in the Bible because a working knowledge of the sixty-five books preceding it is the basic requirement for an understanding of its vivid language. I get a little irritated when I see a new Christian immediately start teaching a class in the Book of Revelation. Why doesn't he go back to the beginning and start with Genesis? Take some other book, but do not *begin* with Revelation. I come to the teaching of Revelation only after having taken nearly five years to go through the rest of the Scriptures. I believe that gives us the right to teach the Book of Revelation; I would not want it otherwise. It was Peter who said, "Knowing this first, that no prophecy of the scripture is of any private interpretation" (2 Pet. 1:20). You do not interpret Revelation by itself; there are sixty-five books before it. The symbols are going to be given to us, but we need to remember that the symbols stand for awful realities.

The opening of the seventh seal introduces the seven trumpets, and that is the way this entire book is built. If the structure of the book is followed, it will prevent you from going off into fanaticism and sensationalism and, as a Christian, it certainly ought to keep you from saying, "The Book of Revelation is so frightful! It terrifies me!" It ought not to terrify you. Actually, it ought to be a comfort to you. I thank God that He is going to judge this world that is running wild today. The way that mankind has blundered and gotten this world into a mess makes it look like it is filled with madmen. I thank God He is going to judge it, and He is going to judge it *rightly*. It is very comforting to recognize that.

People often urge me to speak out on my radio broadcast against certain things that are taking place. It is not my business to get on radio and denounce every wrong. My business is to give out just the Word of God, and that is what I am going to do. *He* is going to straighten this world out someday. I wouldn't have that job for anything in the world. I am glad it is His job. He is going to straighten out this world, and He is going to move in judgment.

Maybe you don't like the fact that the gentle Jesus is going to judge. We have already seen that the wrath of the Lamb will be terrifying to those on earth. My friend, when you talk about the gentle Jesus, you had better get acquainted with Him. He died for you, He loves you, and He wants to save you, but if you will not have Him, I tell you, there is waiting ahead of you a terrifying judgment. Someone will say to me, "You are trying to frighten people." I would like to scare you into heaven if I could, but I know you are too sophisticated and cynical for that. But, my beloved, *judgment is coming on this earth*. I say, Hallelujah! I am glad that it is coming and that God is not going to let the world go on like it is now. It has gone on long enough.

OPENING OF THE SEVENTH SEAL—INTRODUCTION OF SEVEN TRUMPETS

The first verse of this chapter describes what takes place as the seventh seal is opened.

> **And when he had opened the seventh seal, there was silence in heaven about the space of half an hour [Rev. 8:1].**

Here is my translation of this verse:

> *And when (ever) He opened the seventh seal there came to pass a silence in heaven of about a half hour.*

"There was silence in heaven about the space of half an hour." Many years ago I was speaking at a conference to about three or four hundred young people here in Southern California. I was out on the grounds of the camp, and coming toward me was a group of girls, and in the middle of them there was one boy. It looked like the girls were going to take him apart, and they were making a great deal of noise about it. Finally, they came up to me, and the girls wanted me to hear what this fellow had said. He said to me, "Dr. McGee, did you know that there are not going to be any women in heaven?"

I said, "No, I didn't know that. Do you have Scripture for it?"

He said, "Yes. The Bible says that there is going to be silence in heaven for the space of half an hour. If there are any women there, there couldn't be any silence for that long!"

That young man was surrounded by a bunch of girls who were attempting to correct him on that particular interpretation, and frankly I agreed with the girls that that is not the meaning here at all. This verse does not mean that there are not going to be any women in heaven!

I probably did wrong to open this passage on that very light note, because here is a passage that has to do with a great solemnity and great seriousness. The Lord Jesus Christ is still in command. He opens the seventh seal, and there is introduced a fanfare of seven trumpets. He directs the action now from heaven. We need to keep that before us through the entire book. Do not lose sight of the fact that Revelation presents Him in His glory as the Judge of all the earth.

It may deceive you to have Him presented as the gentle Jesus who went about doing good—which He did, but we are also going to see the *wrath* of the Lamb some day. The Lamb is the One of whom John the Baptist said, ". . . Behold the Lamb of God, which taketh away the sin of the world" (John 1:29). Men are not lost because they are sinners; they are lost because they have rejected Jesus who died for them. Even if you go into a lost eternity and have not accepted Christ, He died for you, and you simply made His sacrifice for you of no avail. You have trodden underfoot the blood of Christ when you take that kind of attitude and position toward Him.

This is a very solemn scene. The Lord Jesus Christ orders a halt on all fronts: heaven, hell, and earth. Nothing can move without his permission. He had already ordered the cessation of natural forces on the earth when He ordered the sealing and saving of two definite groups. Now, for a brief moment, there is a lull in judgment activity; there is a heavenly hush. Godet defined it: "This silence is a pause of action." It is the lull before the storm.

Why is there this strange silence? God's patience is not exhausted. When the sixth seal was opened and nature responded with a mighty convulsion, brave men weakened for a moment. Christ gave them opportunity to repent. But like the Pharaoh of old who, when the heat was taken off, let his willful heart return to its original intention, many men will go back to their blasphemous conduct when there is a calm. They probably will even rebuke themselves for showing a yellow streak. They will say, "It was only nature reacting. It wasn't God, after all. Everything can be explained by natural causes." This, my friend, is the lull before the storm. As someone has said, "The steps of God from mercy to judgment are always slow, reluctant, and measured." God is reluctant to judge for He is slow to anger. Judgment is His strange work. Isaiah writes: "For the LORD shall rise up as in mount Perazim, he shall be wroth as in the valley of Gibeon, that he may do his work, his strange work; and bring to pass his act, his strange act" (Isa. 28:21).

What is strange about God? That He judges, that He is a God of love, judging His creatures. "For I have no pleasures in the death of him that dieth, saith the Lord GOD . . ." (Ezek. 18:32). This silence marks the transition from grace to judgment. God is waiting. By the way, He is waiting for you today if you have not come to Him. You *can* come to Him, for He is a gracious Savior.

BLOWING OF THE SEVEN TRUMPETS

Judgment is getting ready to come upon the earth. This is the lull before the storm of judgment which is coming on the earth during this particular period. When I was a boy, my dad built a storm cellar wherever we moved. I spent half of my boyhood, during the spring and early summer, sleeping in the storm cellar. Late one evening my dad and I were standing in the storm cellar doorway. He was watching a storm come up, and he saw that it was not going to hit our little town in southern Oklahoma. It hit one just about ten miles away. We could see the funnel as it let down near that little town. But before that storm hit, there was a certain stillness. The wind had been blowing, the rain had been coming down, there had been a great deal of thunder and lightning, but suddenly all of that stopped, and for a few moments there was a deathlike silence. Then the wind began to blow like I've never seen it blow. It was not a funnel-shaped hurricane or a tornado, but just a straight wind. It was all my dad could do to get that storm cellar door down, and I helped him hold onto the chain. The storm broke in all its fury. This is the way the Great Tribulation will break upon the earth, and it is presented to us in this way in the blowing of the trumpets, which is the subject of chapter 8, verse 2, through chapter 11.

ANGEL AT THE ALTAR WITH CENSER OF INCENSE

And I saw the seven angels which stood before God; and to them were given seven trumpets [Rev. 8:2].

And I saw the seven angels who stand before God, and there was given to them seven (war) trumpets.

These "seven angels" are introduced to us as a special group. I believe that Gabriel is in this group because we are told that he stood before God. When he announced the birth of John the Baptist to Zacharias, he said, ". . . I am Gabriel, that stand in the presence of God . . ." (Luke 1:19). The seraphim are also identified as beings who stand before God (see Isa. 6:1–2). However, these seven angels are seemingly a different order from the seraphim as their mission and service are altogether different.

"Seven trumpets" have a special meaning for Israel. I don't want you to miss this; I consider this all important. Here is where it is essential to have a knowledge of the Old Testament. In the Book of Numbers, Moses was given instructions by God for the making of two silver trumpets. Two was the number of witnesses. The Lord has said on several occasions that in the mouth of two witnesses a matter would be established. These two trumpets were used on the wilderness march in a twofold way. They were used for the calling of the assembly, and they were used to start the procession moving on the wilderness march. "Make thee two trumpets of silver; of a whole piece shalt thou make them: that thou mayest use them for the calling of the assembly, and for the journeying of the camps" (Num. 10:2).

When Israel entered the land, the trumpets were used for two other purposes: "And if ye go to war in your land against the enemy that oppresseth you, then ye shall blow an alarm with the trumpets; and ye shall be remembered before the LORD your God, and ye shall be saved from your enemies. Also in the day of your gladness, and in your solemn days, and in the beginnings of your months, ye shall blow with the trumpets over your burnt offerings, and over the sacrifices of your peace offerings; that they may be to you for a memorial before your God: I am the LORD your God" (Num. 10:9–10).

A single trumpet was blown on the wilderness march to assemble the princes: "And if they blow but with one trumpet, then the princes, which are heads of the thousands of Israel, shall gather themselves unto thee" (Num. 10:4).

This single trumpet is, to my judgment, that which corresponds to "the last trump" which Paul mentions in 1 Corinthians 15. This trumpet was for the bringing together of a certain group out of Israel. Paul writes: "Behold, I shew you a mystery; We shall not all sleep, but we shall all be changed, In a moment, in the twinkling of an eye, at the last trump: for the trumpet shall sound, and the dead shall be raised incorruptible, and we shall be changed" (1 Cor. 15:51–52).

Unfortunately, there are some who assume that "the last trump" of 1 Corinthians 15 is the seventh trumpet of Revelation—there is no relation at all. Listen again to Paul: "For the Lord himself shall descend from heaven with a shout, with the voice of the archangel, and with the trump of God: and the dead in Christ shall rise first" (1 Thess. 4:16).

The "shout" is the voice of the Lord Jesus. "The voice of the archangel" means that His voice is *like* that of an archangel. "The trump of God" is still His voice—His voice will sound like a trumpet. We see that from chapter 1, verse 10, where John says that he heard a voice like the sound of a trumpet, and he turned to see the glorified Christ. The glorified Christ is going to call His own out of the earth. When Paul speaks of "the last trump"—"the trumpet shall sound, and the dead shall be raised"—he means the call of the Lord Jesus. It is the last call that He makes to the church, and it is therefore called "the last trump." But the Old Testament type of it is the calling of the princes from out of the children of Israel. One trumpet is blown, and it has no relation to the movement of the children of Israel on the wilderness march.

However, the trumpets did sound an alarm which moved Israel on the wilderness march, and an alarm was sounded to move each division. The tribes were divided into four groups of three tribes each which camped on the four sides of the tabernacle. In addition there were three separate families of Levi who carried the articles of furniture of the tabernacle: Kohath, Gershon, and Merari. Four and three make *seven*. There were seven blowings of the trumpets to move Israel out. When the first trumpet was blown, the ark moved out with the Kohathites carrying it. Then the tribe of Judah moved out with the two other tribes under the banner of Judah, and so on until they were all on the march. Every man knew his place and stayed in his station. There was no disorder in the camp of Israel whatsoever. (The apostle Paul says that everything is to be done decently and in order in the church. I wish the church were as orderly as Israel was on the wilderness march.) But note particularly that it took *seven trumpets* to move them out.

The seven trumpets of Revelation will likewise have the positive effect of moving Israel into the land of Palestine. I believe that it will take these seven trumpets to get all of Israel back into that land. This is another reason I do not believe their present return to the land is a fulfillment of prophecy. Rather, it will be fulfilled in the Great Tribulation with the blowing of the seven trumpets as they were on the wilderness march. After the seventh trumpet, Israel is identified for us in chapter 12 as the special object of God's protection. An understanding of the trumpets, therefore, will prevent us from identifying "the last trump" of the church with the seven trumpets of Revelation.

As the trumpets of Israel were used at the battle of Jericho, so the walls of this world's opposition to God will crumble and fall during the Great Tribulation. When the Lord Jesus comes, He will put down the last vestige of rebellion against Himself and against God and establish His kingdom here upon this earth. This is a book of triumph and of victory for our God. At the end it has the Hallelujah Chorus, and maybe you and I can sing it when we get there!

> **And another angel came and stood at the altar, having a golden censer; and there was given unto him much incense, that he should offer it with the prayers of all saints upon the golden altar which was before the throne [Rev. 8:3].**
>
> *And another angel came and stood over* [Gr.: *epi*] *the altar, having a golden censer (bowl); and there was given unto him much incense, that he should add it unto (give it unto) the prayers of all the saints upon the golden altar which was before the throne.*

"Another angel" is positively not Christ. The Lord Jesus Christ is no longer in the position of intercessor for the church. We saw in chapters 4—5 that He moved away from that position and was given the seven-sealed book. He is in charge of everything that happens from there on in Revelation. He is not moving as one of the actors down on earth's stage; He is in heaven with the church, and He is not the intercessor. He is now in the place of judgment. He holds the book of the seven seals, and He directs all the activities from the throne. This angel is, as it is stated here, just "another angel." I do not think the Lord Jesus would be identified as that. Although it is true that in the Old Testament the preincarnate Christ appeared as an angel, I do not believe He will ever appear again as an angel. He will be as He is in the glorified body, and we will see Him as He is someday.

The "golden altar" is the place where prayer is offered. Christ is not in the place of intercession before the golden altar. He is now upon the throne. Incense is likened unto prayer and is a type of prayer. David said in Psalm 141:2, "Let my prayer be set forth before thee as incense. . . ."

Incense speaks of the value of Christ's name and work in prayer. "If you ask in My name" is His injunction. Many today who really believe the Word of God are falling into the habit of ending their prayer by just saying "Amen." Someone said to me, "It is redundant to say, 'In Jesus' name,' because in your heart you are praying in Jesus' name." I agree that to pray in Jesus' name means more than simply putting on a tag end, "in Jesus' name." But I want to say that if you are making a prayer in Jesus' name, and especially a public prayer, be sure to say that it is in Jesus' name. I believe that is very important. Here they are offering incense, a sweet smelling incense. You and I are not heard for our much speaking or for our flowery prayer. We are heard when our prayer is made in Jesus' name.

It is interesting that the incense was given to this angel. Christ didn't need anything given to Him when He prayed. The prayers of saints which were offered under the fifth seal (see Rev. 6:9–11) are now being answered because of the person and sacrifice of Christ.

> **And the smoke of the incense, which came with the prayers of the saints, ascended up before God out of the angel's hand [Rev. 8:4].**
>
> *And the smoke of the incense, with the prayers of the saints, went up before God out of the angel's hand.*

Prayer is going to be answered because of Christ.

> **And the angel took the censer, and filled it with fire of the altar, and cast it into the earth: and there were voices, and thunderings, and lightnings, and an earthquake [Rev. 8:5].**
>
> *And the angel hath taken (takes) the censer, and filled it with the fire of the altar, and he throws (casts) it upon (into) the earth: and there were (came to pass) thunders, and voices, and lightnings, and an earthquake.*

The high priest of Israel took a censer with him as he carried the blood into the Holy of Holies. Here the ritual is reversed, because out of heaven the censer is hurled upon the earth. In other words, the prayers ascended as incense, and now we have the answer coming down. The

Tribulation saints had prayed, "Oh, God, avenge us!" The people of the earth, having rejected the death of Christ for the judgment of their sins, must now bear the judgment for their own sins. The Great Tribulation is going to get under way.

"Thunders" denotes the approach of the coming storm of God's judgment.

"Voices" reveals that this is the intelligent direction of God and not the purposeless working of natural forces. God is in charge.

"Lightnings" follow the thunder. This is not a reversal of the natural order. We see the lightning before we hear the thunder due to the fact that light waves move faster than sound waves. Actually, the thunder comes first, but we do not hear it until after we have already seen the lightning.

The "earthquake" is the earth's response to the severe pressure which will be placed upon it during the judgment of the Great Tribulation Period.

And the seven angels which had the seven trumpets prepared themselves to sound [Rev. 8:6].

And the seven angels having the seven trumpets prepared themselves that they should blow the trumpets.

This is a solemn moment. The half hour of silence is over. The prayers of the saints have been heard. The order is issued to prepare to blow. The angels come to attention, and at the blowing of the trumpets, divine wrath is visited upon rebellious men. The blowing of the trumpets does not introduce *symbols* or *secrets*. The plagues here are *literal* plagues. This method today of evaporating the meaning of Scripture by calling it symbolic is just as bad as denying the inspiration of the Word of God. In other words, it is saying that God doesn't mean what He says but that He means something else altogether.

FIRST TRUMPET—TREES BURN

The first angel sounded, and there followed hail and fire mingled with blood, and they were cast upon the earth:

and the third part of trees was burnt up, and all green grass was burnt up [Rev. 8:7].

And the first angel blew the trumpet, and there followed hail and fire, mingled in blood, and they were cast into the earth and the third part of the earth was burnt up, and the third part of the trees was burnt up, and all the green grass was burnt up.

This is a direct judgment from God. Judgment falls upon plant life, from the grass to the great trees. Every form of botanical life is affected first. Notice, however, that it is only one-third, but it makes a tremendous impact upon the earth. Fire, the great enemy, is the instrument God uses. The Flood was used in the first global judgment; now it is going to be fire. This earth is to be purifed by fire. The forests and the prairies covered with grass are partially destroyed by fire. One-third of the earth denotes the wide extent of the damage. "One-third" means not one-fourth or one-half; it means one-third. Plant life was the first to be created, and it is the first to be destroyed. In the record given in Genesis 1:11, God began with the creation of plant life after order had been brought into the physical globe.

This is a *literal* judgment upon plant life in the same way that the seventh plague of Egypt was literal (see Exod. 9:18–26). I called attention before to the fact that there is a striking similarity between the plagues in Egypt and the trumpet judgments—this is no accident. If you go back to the Book of Exodus, you will see that the plagues are literal—every believer in the Bible has to grant that; then you must also grant that these plagues in Revelation should be taken in the same fashion. I do not know by what flip-flop method of hermeneutics you could interpret one way in one passage and another way in another passage—unless the Scripture makes it clear that you can do such a thing. When hail came down on Egypt, we are told that ". . . the hail smote every herb of the field, and brake every tree of the field" (Exod. 9:25)—it was 100 percent destruction in Egypt; it will be one-third of the earth.

SECOND TRUMPET—SEAS BECOME BLOOD

And the second angel sounded, and as it were a great mountain burning with fire was cast into the sea: and the third part of the sea became blood;

And the third part of the creatures which were in the sea, and had life, died; and the third part of the ships were destroyed [Rev. 8:8–9].

And the second angel sounded (blew the trumpet), and as it were a great mountain burning with fire was thrown (cast) into the sea, and the third of the sea became blood; and there died the third of the creatures which were in the sea, (even) they that have life. And the third of the ships was destroyed.

The sea, which occupies most of the earth's surface, is next affected by this direct judgment of God. The separation of the land and the sea occurred on the same day in which plant life appeared (see Gen. 1:9–10).

I want you to notice the exact language used here. John does not say that a burning mountain was cast into the sea but rather he indicates that a great mass or force "as it were a great mountain burning with fire was [*thrown*] cast into the sea"—*as it were* a great mountain. This careful distinction in the use of language should be noted, especially since it is the common practice to lump together everything in Revelation and call it symbolic. You might think that it gets you out of a lot of trouble, but it gets you out of the frying pan into the fire, by the way.

The mountain represents something as literal and tangible as that which we have in Jeremiah 51:25 where the Lord is talking about Babylon: "Behold, I am against thee, O destroying mountain, saith the LORD, which destroyest all the earth: and I will stretch out mine hand upon thee, and roll thee down from the rocks, and will make thee a burnt mountain."

This literal mass falls into the literal sea, one-third becomes literal blood, and one-third of all the literal living creatures in the literal sea die a literal death. Nothing could be plainer than this. Also, one-third of the literal ships of all literal nations are literally destroyed. If we just let John say what he wants to, he makes it very clear.

There is no use to try to find some symbol. John doesn't say that this is symbolic. He makes it very clear that a great mass, a force, is put into the ocean. I do not know what this could possibly be, and there are two reasons for that. First of all, John didn't tell me; he didn't tell anybody, and therefore, I do not think that anyone has the answer. The second reason is that I don't expect to be here at that time to be reading the evening papers. The bad news that we get in the papers and on television today will continue, only more so, during the Great Tribulation. I won't be here to see it. Therefore, this does not concern me too much, other than it is an awful tragedy that is coming on a Christ-rejecting world which actually ridicules the Word of God today. This is something that certainly makes the believer sorrowful in his heart—but it ought to do more than that. It not only ought to affect our hearts; it ought also to affect our wills and our feet to start us moving to get the Word of God out to the world. That is our responsibility, and I believe it is a very solemn responsibility. We cannot keep this judgment from coming to earth, but we *can* get the Word of God out and reduce the population that will be left on the earth so that fewer people will go through that terrible time.

THIRD TRUMPET—FRESH WATERS BECOME BITTER

And the third angel sounded, and there fell a great star from heaven, burning as it were a lamp, and it fell upon the third part of the rivers, and upon the fountains of waters;

And the name of the star is called Wormwood: and the third part of the waters became wormwood; and many men died of the waters, because they were made bitter [Rev. 8:10–11].

And the third angel blew the trumpet (sounded), and a great star burning as a torch fell from (out of) heaven, and it fell upon the third part of the rivers, and upon the fountains of the waters; and the name of the star is called Wormwood [Gr.: Apsinthos]; and the third part of the waters became wormwood; and many men died of the waters, because they were made bitter.

We are living in a world today where a great deal is being said about pollution, and it is a real problem. Man seems to have gotten a head start on the star in polluting all the waters. Personally, I think that man is going to be forced to clean up the water of the world if he is going to be able to exist at all. Self-preservation is considered to be the first law of nature, and man wants to hang on to this little earth; so he's going to do something about it. In the Great Tribulation, the fresh water is polluted, and the drinking water for mankind is contaminated, that is, one-third of it is.

Those of us who live in Southern California know something of the scarcity of fresh water for drinking and domestic use. I am told that in Los Angeles it costs somewhere around $100 million just to turn on the spigot to get the water here to us. Fresh water is something that is essential for man and beast. I remember the drought of the '50s in Dallas, Texas. The city's water supply came from man-made lakes; the lakes dried up, and the supply was exhausted. It was necessary to get water from the Red River, but the oil companies had allowed salt water from their deep wells to drain into the river. Nobody worried about it until they needed the water for drinking. It was so salty, it was barely possible to drink it. Many people traveled to surrounding little towns to get a bottle of water to bring home. These experiences teach man how dependent he is upon fresh water.

When the children of Israel crossed over the Red Sea, they came to Marah where the waters were bitter. Moses was directed to take a tree and cast it into the waters to make them sweet. Here in Revelation, the sweet waters are made bitter by a meteor, a star out of heaven. The tree that Moses put into the water speaks of the cross of Christ.

"Wormwood" is a name used metaphorically in the Old Testament, according to Vincent (*Word Studies in the New Testament*, vol. 2, p. 506), in the following ways: (1) idolatry of Israel (see Deut. 29:18); (2) calamity and sorrow (see Jer. 9:15; 23:15; Lam. 3:15, 19); and (3) false judgment (see Amos 5:7).

This star is literal and is a meteor containing poison which contaminates one-third of the earth's fresh water supply. The star's name suggests that this is a judgment upon man for idolatry and injustice. Calamity and sorrow are the natural compensations that are coming upon man because of this judgment.

FOURTH TRUMPET—SUN, MOON, AND STARS SMITTEN

And the fourth angel sounded, and the third part of the sun was smitten, and the third part of the moon, and the third part of the stars; so as the third part of them was darkened, and the day shone not for a third part of it, and the night likewise [Rev. 8:12].

And the fourth angel blew the trumpet (sounded), and the third part of the sun was smitten, and the third of the moon, and the third of the stars; in order that a third part of them might be darkened, and the day not shine for the third part of it, and the night in like manner.

Another phase of creation upon which mankind on this earth is solely dependent for light and life is the sun. To a lesser degree, man is dependent on the moon and stars. It was on the fourth day of recreation that these heavenly bodies appeared. They had been created before, but the light broke through on the fourth day. Now the light is put out, as it were, over a third part of the earth. God let these lights break through, the greater light to rule the day, the lesser light to rule the night, and they were to be for signs and seasons. The Lord Jesus indicated that in the Great Tribulation there would be special signs in these heavenly bodies: "Immediately after the tribulation of those days shall the sun be darkened, and the moon shall not give her light, and the stars shall fall from heaven, and the powers of the heavens shall be shaken" (Matt. 24:29).

The laws of nature are radically altered by these disturbances. There is a definite limitation—only a third part of the light and of the day is affected. The intensity of the light has the wattage reduced by one-third. Talk about an energy shortage! Believe me, my friend, one is coming to this earth someday.

I saw an arresting billboard in Seattle, Washington, when Boeing had shut down many of its plants, laid off several thousand men, and people were beginning to leave town. On this billboard on Highway 5, some wag put this sign: "The last one leaving town, please turn out the lights." Well, God is getting ready to turn out the lights here on this earth. However, the Lord has made it clear, "While the earth remaineth, seedtime and harvest, cold and heat, and summer and winter, and day and night shall not cease" (Gen. 8:22).

A statement from Robert Govett (*The Apocalypse Expounded by Scripture,* p. 180) is intensely interesting in this connection, in view of present-day efforts to eliminate the death penalty:

> Hence day continues still, though its brightness is diminished. God shows His right to call in question man's right to the covenant. He has not kept the terms. Blood for blood is not shed by the nations. By this time the command to put the murderer to death is, through a false philanthropy, refused by the world.

This is another angle to the question of capital punishment. These judges with soft heads as well as soft hearts eliminate capital punishment and turn the criminals loose on us in this world today. Man continues to move in that direction, but God says, "I gave you a covenant that you were to protect human life, and you are protecting human life when you execute murderers." Capital punishment is a deterrent to crime, and any person who says it is not a deterrent to crime must be like an ostrich with his head in the sand. I think that capital punishment will be abolished by Antichrist if it is not done so before.

> **And I beheld, and heard an angel flying through the midst of heaven, saying with a loud voice, Woe, woe, woe, to the inhabiters of the earth by reason of the other voices of the trumpet of the three angels, which are yet to sound! [Rev. 8:13].**
>
> *And I saw and heard one eagle, flying in mid-heaven (the meridian), saying with a great voice* [Gr.: *phōne megale*], *Woe, woe, woe to them dwelling upon the earth, by reason of the remaining voices of the trumpet of the three angels who are about to blow the trumpet (sound).*

When the fourth trumpet is blown, the announcement is made of a peculiar intensity of woe and judgment that is coming on the earth. The last three trumpets are separated from the other four; they are "woe" trumpets.

"And I saw and heard one eagle." Somebody says, "This eagle is *talking!* Is it a literal eagle?" My friend, if God can make a parrot and a few other birds talk, I do not think He will have any problem at all with an eagle.

It is interesting to note that our Lord used the eagle to speak of His coming: "For wheresoever the carcase is, there will the eagles be gathered together" (Matt. 24:28)—that is after the great Battle of Armageddon.

CHAPTER 9

THEME: *The fifth and sixth trumpets*

The last three trumpets are separated from the other four by the fact that they are three woe trumpets. My translation of chapter 8, verse 13, reads, "And I saw and heard one eagle, flying in midheaven, saying with a great voice, Woe, woe, woe to them dwelling upon the earth, by reason of the remaining voices of the trumpet of the three angels who are about to blow the trumpet." We are coming to a section that is weird and wild; it boggles the mind as we read through this chapter. All kinds of interpretations have been given of this section. But let us get our feet back on the ground, and we will find that the things mentioned here ought not to frighten us. If you are a child of God, you are not going through these things. It is not the "blessed hope" of the church to endure these things. The church will have been taken out of the world by this time, and these are the things which will happen in the Great Tribulation Period to a Christ-rejecting world.

These woes mark the deepest darkness and the most painful intensity of the Great Tribulation Period. They are generally associated with the last three and one-half years of the Seventieth Week of Daniel, which is the Great Tribulation Period. These will be the blackest days in human history.

The language used in this section is admittedly the most difficult of interpretation, but this does not preclude our policy of following the literal line, even when the figures adopted are the most vivid and wild. If another interpretation is proper, John will furnish us the key.

FIFTH TRUMPET—FALLEN STAR AND PLAGUE OF LOCUSTS

Here in verse 1 we have a description of the scene as the fifth angel sounds a trumpet and a star falls from heaven.

And the fifth angel sounded, and I saw a star fall from heaven unto the earth: and to him was given the key of the bottomless pit [Rev. 9:1].

And the fifth angel sounded (blew the trumpet), and I saw a star out of heaven fallen into the earth, and there was given to him a key of the long shaft (pit, well) of the abyss.

Notice the proper meaning of "the bottomless pit" is the long shaft (or pit or well) of the abyss.

"I saw a star fall from heaven unto the earth." We have already seen two stars, and we said that they were literal stars, meteors, that fall to the earth. I recall several years ago sitting with my wife on a lanai of a hotel on Waikiki Beach and watching a shower of meteors or shooting stars. Meteors are the shooting stars which we see on a summer night. But here we have a different kind of star because it is called "him" and acts with intelligence. We are talking now about an unusual person. This star is different, therefore, from the stars mentioned at the sounding of the fourth trumpet. This star not only acts with intelligence, but he is given a key which he uses—no inanimate star could do this.

We believe that this star is Satan. Some have identified this star as Antichrist; if this is so, it lends support to the view that Antichrist is Satan incarnate, but I do not accept that. My point is that Antichrist is exactly that: he is everything Christ is not, and he is motivated by Satan. The reasons for interpreting this star as Satan are abundant. The prophet Isaiah writes: "How art thou fallen from heaven, O Lucifer, son of the morning! how art thou cut down to the ground, which didst weaken the nations!" (Isa. 14:12).

In Luke's Gospel we read: "And he [Jesus] said unto them, I beheld Satan as lightning fall from heaven" (Luke 10:18).

That would be like a fallen star, you see. Also, Paul writes: "And no marvel; for Satan himself is transformed into an angel of light" (2 Cor. 11:14). These Scriptures confirm the position that Satan is in view here. John will state later that Satan was put out of heaven and cast to the earth (see Rev. 12:7–9). If we have established the fact that the "star" is Satan being cast out of heaven, then what does he do? He goes down and takes the key to the abyss, which apparently means that God is permitting him to do so. A key denotes authority and power, and this is given to him of God; it is the permissive will of God.

"The long shaft of the abyss" means the long shaft leading to the abyss. The abyss is the bottomless pit which will be seen in chapter 20, verse 3. The abyss and hades may be synonymous terms, but the abyss and hell are not the same. Our Lord probably referred to the abyss in Matthew 12:40: "For as Jonas was three days and three nights in the whale's belly; so shall the Son of man be three days and three nights in the heart of the earth."

The Lord speaks here of His descent into the "heart of the earth." The body of Jesus was not actually buried in the earth—it was put in a new tomb—and it certainly was not in the *heart* of the earth. Rather, what we have in this language of Matthew is that He went to the abyss, which apparently is hades or sheol. When the Lord Jesus told about the deaths of the rich man and Lazarus (see Luke 16:19–31), He made it quite obvious that hades is in two compartments. The rich man died and went to the place of torment. The poor man died and went into Abraham's bosom, or paradise as our Lord called it. The Lord went down there in His death to announce to the saved His victory and that He would be leading them into the presence of God. That is, I believe, what Paul meant when he said that the Lord Jesus ". . . led captivity captive . . ." (Eph. 4:8). He went to the abyss to announce that His redemption had been wrought.

It behooves us not to be dogmatic where the Scriptures are silent, but there is the thought that a shaft leads from the surface of the earth to the heart of the earth. I know that may sound very much like I am being superstitious. I do accept this idea, but I would not be dogmatic about it. If you have some advance information and can prove to me that it means something else, I would certainly be glad to accept it.

The Lord now holds the key to the abyss (see Rev. 1:18). Peter tells us the demons are imprisoned there (see 2 Pet. 2:4). In Luke 8:30–31 we read: "And Jesus asked him, saying, What is thy name? And he said, Legion: because many devils were entered into him. And they besought him that he would not command them to go out into the deep [abyss]."

The abyss is a very literal place. The idea that heaven and hell are mythological and that heaven is a beautiful isle of somewhere, a Shangri-la, hanging out in space, is not the teaching of the Word of God. The teaching of the Word of God is that heaven is as literal as the place where you live today and that hell is equally as real as the place where you now live.

During the last part of the Great Tribulation, the key to the abyss is given to Satan, and he is given a freedom that he never has had before. I believe this explains why men cannot die during this period. Satan wants to keep them alive; he does not want his army decimated at all.

And he opened the bottomless pit; and there arose a smoke out of the pit, as the smoke of a great furnace; and the sun and the air were darkened by reason of the smoke of the pit [Rev. 9:2].

And he opened the long shaft (pit, well) of the abyss, and there came smoke out of the long shaft of the abyss as the smoke of a great furnace; and the sun and the air were darkened from the smoke of the shaft of the abyss.

Out of the shaft, like a great erupting volcano, will come smoke to cover the entire earth. This is smog of the most vicious type. The literal interpretation of this verse is the correct and most satisfying one.

And there came out of the smoke locusts upon the earth: and unto them was given power, as the scorpions of the earth have power.

And it was commanded them that they should not hurt the grass of the earth, neither any green thing, neither any tree; but only those men which have not the seal of God in their foreheads [Rev. 9:3–4].

> *And out of the smoke came forth locusts upon the earth, and power was given to them as the scorpions of the earth have power. And it was said to them in order that they should not hurt the grass of the earth nor any green things, nor any tree, but only (except) the men who do not have the seal of God on their foreheads.*

To me this beggars description. John uses symbolic language which describes creatures so frightful that this is the only way he could speak of them.

These are locusts, but they are of a very unusual character. As Govett remarks (*The Apocalypse Expounded by Scripture*, pp. 185–186), they are "no common locusts," and he gives the following reasons:

(1) for they eat no vegetable productions;
(2) the locusts of the earth have no king (Prov. 30:27); these have;
(3) in the plague of Egypt the inspired recorder had said, "Before them there were no such locusts as they, neither after them shall be such" (Exod. 10:14);
(4) yet they are literal creatures resembling the literal animals named: the lion, the horse, the scorpion, the man.

This is a plague of locusts which is as literal as the plague of locusts in Egypt. Joel prophesied of a coming plague of locusts (see Joel 1). Again, a working knowledge of the Old Testament is essential to the understanding of Revelation. The difference between the locusts here and the locusts in Joel is the character of the locusts and the object of their destruction. They sting as scorpions, and their objects are evil men.

> **And to them it was given that they should not kill them, but that they should be tormented five months: and their torment was as the torment of a scorpion, when he striketh a man [Rev. 9:5].**

And it was given to them in order that they should not kill them, but in order that they should be tormented five months; and their torment was as the torment of a scorpion, when it striketh at man.

The scorpion is shaped like a lobster and lives in damp places. His sting is in his tail; though it is not fatal, it is very painful indeed. This is the picture we are given here. These were mentioned by Joshua when he spoke of the hornet, "And I sent the hornet before you, which drove them out from before you . . ." (Josh. 24:12). Therefore you can see that believers, living during the Great Tribulation who will be acquainted with the Old Testament, will understand what John is talking about regarding these scorpions.

And in those days shall men seek death, and shall not find it; and shall desire to die, and death shall flee from them [Rev. 9:6].

And in those days shall the men seek death, and shall not find it; and they shall earnestly desire to die, and death fleeth from them.

Satan is given the key to this long shaft (which evidently is what is called sheol in the Old Testament and hell [hades] in the New Testament). The shaft leads to the abyss where the spirits of the dead of the ages past have gone. This is where the Lord Jesus went to announce the redemption that He had wrought on the cross. Satan does not want his crowd to die, and it is only his crowd that are attacked by these locusts. Men during this period try to commit suicide and are unable to do it—this reveals something of the awfulness of that day. Satan wants them here because there is a battle between light and darkness that is being waged. There are others who think that maybe it is God who will not let these men die because sinful man must face the consequences of his rebellion—there is no escape. It is not a laughing matter to reject Jesus Christ; it is not a simple thing to ignore Him. People say there are so many important things in this life—and I am willing to grant that many things take second, third, and fourth place—but the most important thing is your decision concerning Jesus Christ.

> **And the shapes of the locusts were like unto horses prepared unto battle; and on their heads were as it were crowns like gold, and their faces were as the faces of men.**
>
> **And they had hair as the hair of women, and their teeth were as the teeth of lions.**
>
> **And they had breastplates, as it were breastplates of iron; and the sound of their wings was as the sound of chariots of many horses running to battle.**
>
> **And they had tails like unto scorpions, and there were stings in their tails: and their power was to hurt men five months [Rev. 9:7–10].**
>
> *And the likenesses of the locusts were like unto horses prepared for war; and on their heads were as it were crowns like gold, and their faces were as the faces of men. And they had hair as the hair of women, and their teeth were as the teeth of lions. And they had breastplates, as it were breastplates of iron; and the sound of their wings was as of chariots of many horses rushing into battle. And they had tails like scorpions, and stings; and in their tails was their power to hurt men five months.*

I am sure you will agree that this is a frightful, weird, and unnatural description. A little closer examination, however, will reveal a striking similarity to the locusts of Palestine, which I think we need to note. Dr. Vincent makes this comment in his book on Revelation:

> The likeness of a locust to a horse, especially to a horse equipped with armor, is so striking that the insect is named in

> German *Heupferd hay-horse*, and in Italian *cavaletta little horse*.

The faces of locusts resemble the faces of men, and the antennae of the locust are compared to a girl's hair. Joel compares the teeth of the locust with those of a lion (see Joel 1:6). Many have commented on the weird sound that the locust makes. In his *Word Studies in the New Testament*, Dr. Vincent quotes Olivier, a French writer:

> It is difficult to express the effect produced on us by the sight of the whole atmosphere filled on all sides and to a great height by an innumerable quantity of these insects, whose flight was slow and uniform, and whose noise resembled that of rain.

There are those today who have attempted to liken this description of the locust to the airplane. I remember as a young fellow hearing a preacher who said that since the sting of the locust is in the tail, it compares to the rear gunner on a bomber! Well, that all sounds very good, but we have now passed from the propeller plane to the jet plane and into the missile age. Maybe you would want to compare these locusts to the missile. Seriously, I do not want to compare it to anything that is known today, because this is not the weapon that is used today but the weapon that is going to be used in the Great Tribulation Period—whatever that is going to be. Our weapons today are so frightful that even Russia and the United States (although they are at opposite poles) are willing to sit down and talk, as long as one thinks the other is as strong or stronger than he is.

"Their power was to hurt men five months." It will be five months of unspeakable agony for those who have been attacked by these unnatural locusts.

> **And they had a king over them, which is the angel of the bottomless pit, whose name in the Hebrew tongue is Abaddon, but in the Greek tongue hath his name Apollyon [Rev. 9:11].**

They have over them (as) king, the angel of the abyss: his name in Hebrew is Abaddon, and in the Greek tongue he hath the name Apollyon.

These locusts are further differentiated from ordinary locusts in that they have a king over them. Proverbs 30:27 says of natural locusts that they have no king. The king or leader of these locusts is probably one of the fallen angels, the chief henchman of Satan, and he is permitted to lead an invasion of earth for the first time. This is something that is going to be rather frightening. His name in Hebrew means "destruction," and in Greek it means "the destroyer." This confirms what Daniel told us, that the demon world of the fallen angels is divided into gradations. I think there are generals, majors, lieutenants, sergeants, and buck privates. In Ephesians we find that the angels of God are divided in the same way.

One woe is past; and, behold, there come two woes more hereafter [Rev. 9:12].

The one woe is past; behold there come yet two woes after these things.

The first woe introduced to us the last half of the Great Tribulation Period, and it had a duration of five months. Apparently, the last two woes will cover the remainder of that period. The warning here indicates that worse things are to follow, and the next trumpet reveals that this was not just an idle warning.

SIXTH TRUMPET—ANGELS LOOSED AT RIVER EUPHRATES

And the sixth angel sounded, and I heard a voice from the four horns of the golden altar which is before God,

Saying to the sixth angel which had the trumpet, Loose the four angels which are bound in the great river Euphrates [Rev. 9:13–14].

And the sixth angel blew (sounded) the trumpet. And I heard one (a single) voice out of the horns of the golden altar which is before God, saying to the sixth angel having the trumpet, loose the four angels which have been bound at the great river Euphrates.

When the sixth angel blew the trumpet, a command came from the horns of the golden altar. That golden altar speaks of prayer; that is what it spoke of in the tabernacle here on earth. This is where the angel offered prayer at the beginning of the blowing of the trumpets (see Rev. 8:3). The sixth angel not only blows the trumpet but is also given a command to loose the four angels bound at the river Euphrates. This angel receives in turn his orders from a voice that was there at the horns of the golden altar. It is the voice of Christ. He has now ripped off the seventh seal which led into the trumpets and which will lead into the seven personalities and the seven bowls of wrath.

The angels who are bound are evidently evil. Why would they be bound if they were not evil? Releasing them turns loose a flood tide of destruction on the earth. They were bound away from the others, I believe, because of the enormity of their crime.

Why were they bound at this particular location at the Euphrates River? Though this is rather difficult to explain, the prominence of this area in Scripture cannot be overlooked. The Garden of Eden was somewhere in this section. The sin of man began here. The first murder was committed here. The first war was fought here. Here was where the Flood began and spread over the earth. Here is where the Tower of Babel was erected. To this area were brought the Israelites of the Babylonian captivity. Babylon was the fountainhead of idolatry. And here is the final surge of sin on the earth during the Great Tribulation Period.

The Euphrates actually marks the division between East and West. It was Kipling who said that East is East and West is West, and never the twain shall meet. That is true to a certain extent. Perhaps there has been a restraining influence in the past which has kept the hordes of the East from spilling over into the West, but it is going to be broken down. It was Napoleon who made the statement: "China is a sleeping giant, and God pity the generation that wakes her up." Well, we woke her up, and she is very much alive today. China represents one-fourth of the world's population. If you take the peoples of the East, of the Orient, beyond the Euphrates River, you have most of the population of the world. Suppose they start moving? My friend, they are going to move someday. From the time of Alexander the Great, the white man has had his day. Colonialism, as far as the white man is concerned, is over now, but communism's colonialism is still on the march. The dark races are awakening. They have been held back, and apparently these four angels had something to do with holding them back.

Zechariah locates Babylon as the last stand of false religion (see Zech. 5). This is where Satan's last stand will take place.

> **And the four angels were loosed, which were prepared for an hour, and a day, and a month, and a year, for to slay the third part of men.**
>
> **And the number of the army of the horsemen were two hundred thousand thousand: and I heard the number of them [Rev. 9:15–16].**
>
> *And the four angels were loosed, who had been prepared for the hour, and day, and month, and year, that they might kill the third of men. And the number of the armies of the cavalry was two ten thousands (myriads) of ten thousands (myriads).*

"And the four angels were loosed, who had been prepared for the hour, and day, and month, and year." You will have to take that literally, my friend, because I do not know how else you would take it. The very hour is marked out.

"That they might kill the third of men." At the blowing of the sixth trumpet, one-third of the population of mankind will be removed. We have already seen a fourth removed, and now a third is removed. Over one-half of the population of the earth will be destroyed in the Great

Tribulation Period. No wonder that the Lord Jesus said, "And except those days should be shortened, there should no flesh be saved . . ." (Matt. 24:22).

The size of the army is stupendous. It is numbered at 200 million. China and India and Japan could easily put that many in the field tomorrow. The great population is in the East today. God help the white man, my friend, when these angels are removed—he will not stand a chance.

What is spoken of here in this passage is the wholesale invasion of the earth by the demon world represented in the locusts. Now they are motivated to a world war. Actually, we have never yet had a real world war in which every nation was involved, but that will take place in the Great Tribulation Period. Are these 200 million human beings? I have so far indicated that they could be, but frankly, I believe that what we have here is the invasion by the demon world, which is a further result of Satan's opening the door of the shaft of the bottomless pit. The following description of these horsemen further confirms this fact.

And thus I saw the horses in the vision, and them that sat on them, having breastplates of fire, and of jacinth, and brimstone: and the heads of the horses were as the heads of lions; and out of their mouths issued fire and smoke and brimstone.

By these three was the third part of the men killed, by the fire, and by the smoke, and by the brimstone, which issued out of their mouths [Rev. 9:17–18].

And, thus (after this manner) I saw the horses in the (my) vision, and those that sat on them, having breastplates as of fire (fiery red), and hyacinth, and brimstone; and the heads of the horses were as the heads of lions; and out of their mouths proceed fire, and smoke and brimstone. By these plagues was the third of men killed, by the fire, by the smoke, and by the brimstone that proceeded out of their mouths.

Many suppose these to be tanks. How do they know that tanks will be used in the Great Tribulation Period? We are talking about a period that is in the future. Modern tanks reveal that this may well be, but I have a notion that they will have something more refined and sophisticated in that period.

Notice that the colors are as striking as the horsemen are unnatural. "Fire" is fiery red; "hyacinth" is the same color as the flower—dull, dark blue; "brimstone" is light yellow.

The horse is the animal of war (see Job 39:19–25). The underworld is now making war on mankind. These creatures from the underworld are unnatural. They are probably demons or demon-controlled. We are given a literal description of them. In his book on Revelation, William R. Newell makes this very timely observation, "Believe, and you scarcely need any comment." The problem with men who come to Revelation and say that it is difficult to understand and impossible to interpret is that they do not believe it. If you simply believe it and read it, it is very clear. Hellish forces will be at work during this period.

These three plagues mentioned here are literal plagues. The fire is literal, the smoke is literal, and the brimstone is literal. The same thing took place at the destruction of Sodom and Gomorrah. I believe this world during the Great Tribulation Period will actually be worse than Sodom and Gomorrah. People talk about homosexuality attaining respectability in our day. Well, it was the accepted life-style in Sodom and Gomorrah, but homosexuals went out of business—God put them out of business. If you think God is going to permit mankind to go into eternity an unnatural creature, you are wrong.

At this point one-third of the population is killed. One-third of nature had already been affected, but mankind had not been touched with a judgment of this magnitude. If the population of the world were 1.5 billion, this would mean that 500 million would be slain. Remember that a fourth part had been slain under the fourth seal. This terrible decimation of the earth's population seemed incongruous with all of history until the atomic bomb fell upon Hiroshima. Since then men have been using more frightening language than that of Revelation. They now talk of the total decimation of earth's inhabitants. But the Lord Jesus said that He will not permit it: ". . . except those days should be shortened, there should no flesh be saved . . ." (Matt. 24:22)—and the human race would commit suicide if it could.

> **For their power is in their mouth, and in their tails: for their tails were like unto serpents, and had heads, and with them they do hurt [Rev. 9:19].**
>
> *For the power of the horses is in their mouths, and in their tails; for their tails are like serpents, having heads, and by them they hurt.*

These are unnatural horses which are able to kill with their mouths. The weirdest feat of all is that, instead of horses' hair for tails, they have serpents which are also used in destroying mankind.

> **And the rest of the men which were not killed by these plagues yet repented not of the works of their hands, that they should not worship devils, and idols of gold, and silver, and brass, and stone, and of wood: which neither can see, nor hear, nor walk:**
>
> **Neither repented they of their murders, nor of their sorceries, nor of their fornication, nor of their thefts [Rev. 9:20–21].**
>
> *And the rest of men who were not killed by these plagues, repented not of the works of their hands, that they should not worship demons, and idols of gold and silver and copper and stone and wood, which can neither see, nor hear, nor walk. Neither repented they of their murders, nor of their sorceries, nor of their fornication, nor of their thefts.*

"Sorceries" is the Greek word *pharmakeion*, from which we get our English word *pharmacy*. *Pharmacy* means "drugs." What were called drugstores when I was a boy are today called pharmacies. The Great Tribulation will be a period when the use of drugs will not be controlled. Drugs will play a large part in the lives of the unsaved and will serve several purposes. Drugs will enable them to bear the judgments of the Great Tribulation Period. I am sure that many a person will turn to drugs when he is stung or bitten by these unnatural creatures. Although they will not die, they will feel like they are going to die, and as a result, they will take drugs to overcome the pain and help them endure the Great Tribulation.

Drugs will also figure largely in the religion of that day. There will be a regular drug culture and drug religion in the days of the Great Tribulation Period. What we are seeing today is very small in comparison to what it will be then. People will resort to everything that will deaden the pain or lift them out of the trouble of that time. Liquor will certainly be very prominent as it is even now. I want to share with you a statement by Dr. J. A. Seiss from his book (*The Apocalypse*, p. 106) published about 1906. The reason I mention the date is that it seems like he wrote it yesterday or that maybe he was preparing it for tomorrow's edition of your local paper. This is his comment on the word *sorceries:*

> We have only to think of the use of alcoholic stimulants, of opium, of tobacco, of the range of cosmetics and medicaments to increase love attractions, of resorts to the pharmacopoeia in connection with sensuality—of the magical agents and treatments alleged to come from the spirit-world for the benefit of people in this—of the thousand impositions in the way of medicines and remedial agents, encouraging mankind to reckless transgression with the hope of easily repairing the damages of nature's penalties—of the growing prevalence of crime induced by these things, setting loose and stimulating to activity the vilest passions, which are eating out the moral sense of society—for the beginnings of that moral degeneracy to which the seer here alludes as characteristic of the period when the sixth trumpet is sounded.

You would think that he had written that for today, but in his day there was no great drug culture nor were drugs and alcohol as big a problem as they are today. Drugs are used today in practically every modern cult which uses sex as a drawing card.

We are told here that they were guilty not only of sorceries, of indulging in drunkenness and in drugs, but also of fornications which lead to thefts. It is alarming the way that adultery is being practiced in the United States. It is promoted as an evidence of our liberty and of the tremendous advancement of civilization! It is interesting that, instead of playing the requiem, this crowd wants to sing and dance and say that the race is improving.

Sorceries and fornication and robbery are going to be increased and a greater emphasis placed upon them. I believe that the Antichrist will use all three of these to bring mankind into subjection to himself. Mankind will be easily lured in that day. Under the influence of drugs, he will accept anything. One of the reasons that our contemporary nightclubs push liquor is not only for the money that is in it, but it also makes their entertainers acceptable. A very inferior singer or comedian goes over well if you've had two cocktails; and if you've had three, then he is a star. Drugs and liquor will put Antichrist over. Paul wrote: "Even him, whose coming is after the working of Satan with all power and signs and lying wonders, And with all deceivableness of unrighteousness in them that perish; because they received not the love of the truth, that they might be saved" (2 Thess. 2:9–10).

I believe that the gospel will go out to every creature before the Rapture, and certainly each one is going to hear it during the Great Tribulation Period. What Paul describes here will only happen to those who have rejected the Word of God. "And for this cause God shall send them strong delusion, that they should believe a lie: That they all might be damned who believed not the truth, but had pleasure in unrighteousness" (2 Thess. 2:11–12).

The moment that you reject the gospel and shut your heart to God, you are wide open for the big lie when it comes. This is the reason so many today fall for everything that comes along. Someone has said that those who stand for nothing will fall for anything. This is it exactly: those today who are not standing for the Word of God are easy prey for the cults.

CHAPTER 10

THEME: *Interlude between the sixth and seventh trumpets*

Chapter 10 is the hiatus, the interlude between the sixth and seventh trumpets. This chapter begins the second of a series of interludes. Between the sixth and seventh seals, there was an interlude as two groups were redeemed and sealed during the Great Tribulation. Here, between the sixth and seventh trumpets, we have an interlude as three personalities are introduced. In this chapter the mighty angel is described, and in the first fourteen verses of chapter 11, the two witnesses are introduced, though not identified.

THE STRONG ANGEL WITH THE LITTLE BOOK

In verse 1 the mighty angel comes from heaven and is introduced.

> **And I saw another mighty angel come down from heaven, clothed with a cloud: and a rainbow was upon his head, and his face was as it were the sun, and his feet as pillars of fire [Rev. 10:1].**

Let me give you my own translation:

> *And I saw another strong (powerful) angel coming down out of heaven clothed with a cloud, and the rainbow was upon his head, and his face was as the sun, and his feet as pillars of fire.*

There has been definite disagreement among outstanding and fundamental Bible expositors as to the identity of the mighty angel. Godet, Vincent, Pettingill, DeHaan, Ironside, Walter Scott, and William Kelly all identify the strong angel as Christ. Newell and others consider him to be just an angel of great power and authority, but not Christ. Dr. John Walvoord takes this viewpoint, and Vernon McGee takes it also. If you go with either crowd, you will be in good company. In the first group are some men I have great respect for and whom I love in the Lord. I have personally known three of those men, and they were my dear friends. If you follow them, it will be all right, and you will be in good company; but if you want to be right, you want to come along with me on this!

There is ample evidence to show that this angel is only a mighty angel. Christ does not appear in Revelation as an angel. It is true that in the Old Testament the preincarnate Christ was seen as *the* Angel of the Lord. But after He took upon Himself our humanity, after He died and rose again and received a glorified body, we now see Him in the place of great power and glory yonder at God's right hand. We never see Him as an angel again. When He was here in His humanity, He was not an angel—He was a man. Therefore, He is revealed in the Book of Revelation as the glorified Christ, as the postincarnate Christ. He is exalted to the nth degree. It is well to keep before us constantly that this book is the unveiling of Jesus Christ. New glories of His person and of His power and performance are unfolding in each chapter. He is now the One judging a Christ-rejecting earth.

"And I saw another strong angel." *Another* means that it is another of the same kind. The other strong angel to whom we were introduced was back in Revelation 5:2. There is no argument there; it is not Christ. It is the livery of this angel (that is, the way in which he is garbed) which has led to identify him as Christ. Though all angels are the servants of Christ, in this final book of the Bible, this is evidently the special envoy of Christ, bearing all the credentials of His exalted position. He comes down out of heaven from the presence of Christ, the One who is in the midst of the throne.

He is "clothed with a cloud." This is his uniform as a special envoy from Christ. The clouds of glory are associated with the second coming of Christ, but the angel described here is not coming in clouds of glory, but he is clothed with a cloud. Furthermore, this is not the second coming of Christ to the earth to establish His kingdom; rather, this angel makes the announcement that He is coming soon. Angels, you recall, announced His first coming, and they will announce His second coming to the earth.

"And the rainbow was upon his head." This is the cap for his uniform and is a reminder of Gods' covenant with man. Although the judgments have come, thick and fast, weird and wild—it beggars language to describe them—this rainbow indicates that God will not send a flood to destroy man again.

"And his face was as the sun." This is his badge of identification. This is the signature of the glorified Christ (see Rev. 1:16). It does not follow that this one must therefore be the Son of God. Moses' face shone after he had been in the presence of God (see Exod. 34:29). This angel's face is shining because he has come out from the presence of Christ. You will recall that the raiment of the angels at the resurrection of Christ also shone (see Luke 24:4). The angel of Revelation 18:1 is a light giver, as the sun and moon, yet no one asserts that he is Christ. Also, I take it that this angel in chapter 10 is not Christ, but he is what it says: an angel, another great, mighty angel.

"And his feet as pillars of fire." This is still part of his uniform. He has come to make a special and solemn announcement of coming judgment. All of these features of identification are his credentials and connect him to the person of Christ as His special envoy. The Lord Jesus is running everything at this particular point. He is the Judge of all the earth.

And he had in his hand a little book open: and he set his right foot upon the sea, and his left foot on the earth,

And cried with a loud voice, as when a lion roareth: and when he had cried, seven thunders uttered their voices [Rev. 10:2–3].

And he had in his hand a little book opened; and he set his right foot upon the sea, and his left foot upon the earth; and he cried with a great voice as (when) a lion roareth: and when he cried the seven thunders spoke their own voices.

There are several reasons that I believe that this little book or scroll is the seven-sealed book which we have seen before. One reason is simply because it is the only book that has been before us, and it is not identified in any other way than it is called "a little book." Frankly, a different word is used here for this book instead of the Greek word *biblion* which is used for the seven-sealed book. But that would not preclude the possibility of its being the same book.

This little book, if it is the same as the seven-sealed book, was originally in the hands of the Father in heaven (see Rev. 5:1). It should be noted how it is first transferred to the nail-pierced hands of God the Son. It was given to the Lord Jesus who was the only One who could open it. The breaking of the seven seals opened the book; and the seven trumpets, six of which have already been blown, are still part of what is in the book. After He removes the seals, the Lord Jesus Christ in turn transfers the book to the angel, who gives it finally to John to eat.

This is the book of the title deed of the earth, and it contains the judgments of the Great Tribulation by which the Lord Jesus is coming to power. The book is now open, and the judgments are on display. This book is the angel's authority for claiming both the sea and the earth for Christ. He puts one foot on the sea and the other foot upon the earth, and he is claiming both for God. In Leviticus 25:23 the Lord gave instructions to Israel concerning the land He had given them: "The land shall not be sold for ever: for the land is mine; for ye are strangers and sojourners with me."

It may be that you think you own a pretty good piece of the real estate of this earth. You hold the title deed. The title has been transferred down through the years to you, and you paid good money for it. You feel it is yours. I say that you are wrong because your title doesn't go back far enough. Sometime in the past, somebody stole it from the Indians. The Indians got it from somebody else—or maybe they just walked in and occupied vacant property. But to whom does it belong? My friend, your property belongs to God, and no matter who you are, you haven't paid Him for it. The earth is His and the fulness thereof (see Ps. 24:1).

God not only claims the land, but He claims the sea as well as the land. "Thou madest him to have dominion over the works of thy hands; thou hast put all things under his feet: All sheep and oxen, yea, and the beasts of the field; The fowl of the air, and the fish of the sea, and whatsoever passeth through the paths of the seas" (Ps. 8:6–8).

God says, "I own the seas also, as well as the land, and I have given this to you. I put man on the earth." Man is a tenant on the earth—some of us haven't paid our rent lately—but we are in a little world that God created. It belongs to Him, and man hasn't been able to pay Him for it yet.

This angel now claims the earth and the sea for the Lord Jesus Christ. When Columbus landed on an island here in the Western Hemisphere, he got off the ship and went to the shore and planted the flag of Spain, claiming the island in the name of the king and queen of the country that had sent him out. That method has been used from time to time. When men came to unoccupied territory, they claimed it. With the title deed of the earth in his hand, and by placing his right foot on the sea and his left foot upon the earth, in a great voice this angel claims all for Christ. The kingdoms of this world *will* become the kingdoms of the Lord Jesus Christ through judgment. As Creator and Redeemer, the world belongs to Him.

The book is described here as "a little book" because the time of the Great Tribulation is not going to be long. We have come here to sort of the halfway mark, and we are going to be told that there is not much more time left. There is not much more to write down, and it has to be a little book. We are told in Romans 9:28: "For he will finish the work, and cut it short in righteousness: because a short work will the Lord make upon the earth."

The Great Tribulation is really a short time. The Lord Jesus said it was a brief time. Daniel labeled it as seven years, which certainly is not long.

The "seven thunders" is God's amen to the angel's claim. Psalm 29:3 says: "The voice of the LORD is upon the waters: the God of glory thundereth: the LORD is upon many waters."

And in Job 37:5 we read: "God thundereth marvellously with his voice; great things doeth he, which we cannot comprehend."

Dr. Vincent makes this very enlightening comment, "The Jews were accustomed to speak of thunder as 'the seven voices.'" In Psalm 29, although it is a brief psalm, "the voice of the LORD" occurs seven times. Israel spoke of thunder as being the voice of the Lord, the seven voices of God.

We need to take time to study these things to find out what they mean instead of trying to cut off the corners, trim them down, and make them fit into some system of prophecy. I am reminded of the lady who went into a shoe store, and when the clerk asked her what size she wore, she replied, "I can get a four on, but really five is my size, but since six feels so good on my foot, I always buy a six!" That is just like some systems of biblical interpretation: they trim Scripture down to fit into the system. Let John mean what he is saying. These seven thunders here are the voice of God. I think it is the voice of the Lord Jesus now in heaven, confirming what this angel has claimed because He is going to come to power on this earth.

> **And when the seven thunders had uttered their voices, I was about to write: and I heard a voice from heaven saying unto me, Seal up those things which the seven thunders uttered, and write them not [Rev. 10:4].**
>
> *And when the seven thunders spoke, I was about to write; and I heard a voice from heaven saying, Seal up the things which the seven thunders spoke and write them not.*

The seven thunders therefore were intelligible. This confirmation was also a statement. John was a scribe, and he was taking down the visions as they were given to him (see Rev. 1:11). He was about to write what the seven thunders had spoken—he heard it, and they were audible words—but he was forbidden to do so. Since this is a book of *revelation*, why is there something concealed? This is the only place in the Book of Revelation where anything is sealed—nothing else is. God makes it very clear at the end of the book that He has told everything. He is not holding back anything from man today. At the end, John writes: "And he saith unto me, Seal not the saying of the prophecy of this book: for the time is at hand" (Rev. 22:10).

Yet this particular message of the seven thunders John is not permitted to write down. This is quite interesting.

If this angel were Christ, John probably would have fallen down and worshiped him. He did so when he saw the glorified Christ in the first chapter of Revelation. Evidently, the reason John did not fall down and worship him was because this is only an angel.

It is a mere assumption to presume to know what the thunders spoke. There are wild speculators who have made ridiculous guesses. Vitringa interpreted the seven thunders as the seven Crusades. Danbuz made them the seven nations which received the Reformation. Elliott believed them to be the pope's bull against Luther. Several of the cults have presumed to reveal the things which were uttered. The Lord Jesus Christ said to John, "Seal them up. Don't write this down." They remain to this day a secret which you don't know, I don't know, and no man knows. If we attempt to say what was spoken, in a few years we will find ourselves to be ridiculous. Why not leave it as it is and draw the lesson from it? Although Jesus Christ is being revealed in this Book, there are a great many things that God is not telling us.

> **And the angel which I saw stand upon the sea and upon the earth lifted up his hand to heaven,**
>
> **And sware by him that liveth for ever and ever, who created heaven, and the things that therein are, and the earth, and the things that therein are, and the sea, and the things which are therein, that there should be time no longer [Rev. 10:5–6].**
>
> *And the angel whom I saw standing upon the sea and upon the earth lifted up his right hand to heaven, and sware by (in) Him that liveth for ever and ever (into the*

ages of the ages), who created heaven and the things in it, and the sea and the things in it, that there shall be no longer delay.

This angel makes it clear that he could not be Christ, since he takes an oath by the eternal Creator. He "lifted up his right hand to heaven, and sware"—he took an oath by the eternal Creator—"by Him that liveth for ever and ever." If he were Christ, he would swear by himself. The writer to the Hebrews says: "For when God made promise to Abraham, because he could swear by no greater, he sware by himself" (Heb. 6:13). God could not swear by anything else because there is none greater than God. The angel swore by another, not by himself, because he is not God, and therefore he is not the Lord Jesus. The Lord Jesus Christ is the eternal God. "In the beginning was the Word, and the Word was with God, and the Word was God. The same was in the beginning with God" (John 1:1–2). We have this statement from the Lord Jesus Himself: "Jesus said unto them, Verily, verily, I say unto you, Before Abraham was, I am" (John 8:58). Christ is the Creator. Listen to John 1:3: "All things were made by him; and without him was not any thing made that was made." In Colossians 1:16 we read: "For by him were all things created, that are in heaven, and that are in earth, visible and invisible, whether they be thrones, or dominions, or principalities, or powers: all things were created by him, and for him." The angel takes an oath in the name of Christ who is in heaven; and as Christ's representative, he claims it all for Christ.

Notice that in my translation I have changed the last part of verse 6 from "that there should be time no longer" to "that there shall be no longer delay." Actually, it does not mean that there shall be time no longer. Rather, this is the glad announcement from heaven to God's saints on earth who are in the midst of all this trouble and who wonder how long it will last. The meaning is that now it will be a very brief time until Christ returns. It is a confirmation of the words of Christ in His Olivet Discourse: "And except those days should be shortened, there should no flesh be saved: but for the elect's sake those days shall be shortened" (Matt. 24:22). The angel is telling the elect that it is not going to be long. He is saying to them, "Don't worry. He that endures to the end, the same shall be saved." Why? Because they are sealed, and they are going to make it through the Great Tribulation Period.

This is likewise in answer to the prayers of the martyrs in Revelation 6:10, and also it is the fulfillment of what we call the Lord's Prayer, "Thy kingdom come" (See Matt. 6:10). The kingdom is coming at this point in time in the Book of Revelation but it does not refer to the time I am writing this. I do not know, and no one on earth knows, whether or not Christ is coming soon.

But in the days of the voice of the seventh angel, when he shall begin to sound, the mystery of God should be finished, as he hath declared to his servants the prophets [Rev. 10:7].

But in the days of the sound of the seventh angel, when he is about to blow (sound the trumpet), and the mystery of God is finished, as He gave the glad tidings to His servants, the prophets.

This all takes place when the seventh angel is preparing to blow the trumpet. This would indicate that the seventh trumpet brings us to the conclusion of the Great Tribulation. It is at this time that the mystery of God is finally made clear. Many single facets of this mystery have been given as the total answer, yet it seems that this is greater than any one and is the sum total of all.

There is a mystery concerning the nation Israel, judgment, suffering, injustice, the silence of God, and the coming kingdom. The basic problem is this: Why did God permit evil, and why has He tolerated it for so long? Do you want to know something? I have studied theology for many years, and I know the answers that men give, but God has not handed in *His* answer yet. He is going to do so someday. There are many things I cannot answer, and I am disturbed that we have some brethren who seem to have all the answers. Candidly, no one has all the answers. As this passage of Scripture indicates, the fact that there is something that we don't know about because it has been sealed means that God has a whole lot to tell us yet. When we get into His presence, we will find out.

May I say this to you: although I do not know the answer to your problem, I know the One who does. I don't have the answer to all my questions either, but I put my hand in His, and He says to me, "My child, walk with Me through the dark. It is going to be all right. We are going to come out into the light, and then you will understand." I suggest that you put your hand into the hand of the One who is your Creator and your Redeemer, very man of very man and very God of very God.

JOHN EATS THE LITTLE BOOK

And the voice which I heard from heaven spake unto me again, and said, Go and take the little book which is open in the hand of the angel which standeth upon the sea and upon the earth [Rev. 10:8].

And the voice which I heard out of heaven, (I heard) it again speaking with me, and saying, Go, take the book which is open in the hand of the angel who standeth upon the sea and upon the earth.

This order comes from Christ in heaven as He is directing every operation recorded in the Book of Revelation. He is in full charge. Revelation is the book that glorifies our wonderful Savior. He is the Judge of all the earth here, and we see Him as God has highly exalted Him and given Him a name above every name. If the voice here is not Christ's, then He has given the order to the angel to speak from heaven.

John has apparently returned to the earth in spirit, because the little book which was formerly in the hand of God the Father is now transferred to John.

And I went unto the angel, and said unto him, Give me the little book. And he said unto me, Take it, and eat it up; and it shall make thy belly bitter, but it shall be in thy mouth sweet as honey.

> **And I took the little book out of the angel's hand, and ate it up; and it was in my mouth sweet as honey: and as soon as I had eaten it, my belly was bitter [Rev. 10:9–10].**
>
> *And I went away to the angel, saying to him, Give to me the little book, and he said to me, Take, and eat it up; and it shall make thy belly bitter, but in thy mouth it shall be as sweet as honey. And I took the little book out of the hand of the angel, and ate it up. And it was in my mouth as sweet as honey. And when I had eaten it, my belly was made bitter.*

John becomes a participant in the great drama which is unfolding before us. He is required to do a very strange thing, one that has a very typical meaning. He eats the little book at the instructions of the angel, and the results are bittersweet. Eating the little book means to receive the Word of God with faith. This is the teaching of the Word of God, for in Jeremiah 15:16 we read: "Thy words were found, and I did eat them; and thy word was unto me the joy and rejoicing of mine heart: for I am called by thy name, O LORD God of hosts." Jeremiah likens the appropriation of the Word to eating it.

Ezekiel does the same thing: "Moreover he said unto me, Son of man, eat that thou findest; eat this roll, and go speak unto the house of Israel. So I opened my mouth, and he caused me to eat that roll. And he said unto me, Son of man, cause thy belly to eat, and fill thy bowels with this roll that I give thee. Then did I eat it; and it was in my mouth as honey for sweetness" (Ezek. 3:1–3). The "roll" here is not a bread roll, but the scroll of that day. Ezekiel said that he ate it, and it was just like cake. That is what the Word of God is to the believer. In Proverbs 16:24 we are told: "Pleasant words are as an honeycomb, sweet to the soul, and health to the bones." In Psalm 119, the psalm which glorifies the Word of God, we find: "How sweet are thy words unto my taste! yea, sweeter than honey to my mouth" (Ps. 119:103).

The part of the Word of God taken by John was judgment. It was sweet because the future is sweet. In Genesis 18:17 we read, "And the LORD said, Shall I hide from Abraham that thing which I do . . . ?" In effect He was saying to Abraham, "We are friends, and I would like to tell you what I am going to do." It is sweet to know what God is going to do, but when you find out that judgment is coming, it is bitter. John eagerly received the Word of God, but when he saw that more judgment was to follow, it brought travail of soul and sorrow of heart. It was sweet in his mouth and bitter in his digestive system. If you and I can take delight in reading this section of the Word of God and the judgments that are to fall upon the earth, then we need to do a great deal of praying to get the mind of God. It is sweet to know the Book of Revelation and what God intends to do, but when we find out that judgment is coming to the Christ-rejecting world around us, we cannot rejoice in that. The prophecy becomes bitter.

There is another very real application of this. Many folk begin the study of prophecy with enthusiasm, but when they find that it is applicable to their life and that it makes demands on them personally, they lose interest, and it becomes a bitter thing. Many people say, "I don't want to hear about the Book of Revelation. I don't like prophecy. It frightens me!" May I say to you that it is supposed to do that, but it should be in your mouth sweet as honey. Unfortunately, there are a lot of people who like to study prophecy because of the natural curiosity to know the future, but they will discover that there is nothing in the Word of God that ministers more to a holy life than the thoughtful study of prophecy. "And every man that hath this hope in him purifieth himself . . ." (1 John 3:3). To be a student of prophecy and live a dirty life will only lead to abnormality. The reason we hear so much abnormality in the interpretation of prophecy in our day is that the Word of God is not having its way in the hearts and lives of the folk who study it. It is unfortunate that people will get interested in prophecy but not in Christian living.

Years ago after I had recently come to California, I went to see Dr. Gaebelein who was visiting here. He said to me, "How do you like your church in California?" I told him, "It's wonderful. I enjoy it, but there is something strange out here. [I have since learned that this is true everywhere, but I had not detected it before.] I can teach the Book of Revelation in my church, and it will fill up on Wednesday nights. But if I teach the Epistle to the Romans, I empty the church." I never shall forget what Dr. Gaebelein said in his broken Prussian accent, "Brother McGee, you are going to find that a great many of the saints are more interested in Antichrist than they are in Christ." I have discovered that he was accurate.

> **And he said unto me, Thou must prophesy again before many peoples, and nations, and tongues, and kings [Rev. 10:11].**
>
> *And they say to me, It is necessary for you to prophesy again against peoples and nations and tongues and kings.*

You can be sure of one thing, that John was properly integrated. He believed that all nations, all peoples, all tongues, and all colors ought to hear the Word of God. They need to hear it because they need to be warned that judgment is coming. If they go through the Great Tribulation, they will soon recognize that it is not the Millennium—in fact, they will feel as if they have entered hell itself. This is the part that made John sad. This is the reason this little book became bitter to John: he must prophesy against many before Christ comes to His kingdom. Much prophecy is to follow. We are not quite halfway through the Book of Revelation. Prophecy about the nations and peoples is necessarily *against* them; it is of judgment to come. This new series of prophecies will begin in chapter 12, and it will reveal the fact that there was a great deal more to say.

My friend, the study of prophecy will have a definite effect upon your life: it will either bring you closer to Christ, or it will take you farther from Him.

CHAPTER 11

THEME: *Interlude between sixth and seventh trumpets; the seventh trumpet blown*

In the first fourteen verses, chapter 11 continues with the interlude between the sixth and seventh trumpets, and in the concluding verses, we have the blowing of the seventh trumpet. In this chapter we learn that forty-two months remain of the Times of the Gentiles and that there are two witnesses who will prophesy for forty-two months. We also have the second woe and then the blowing of the seventh trumpet.

This chapter brings us back to Old Testament ground. The temple, the dealing with time periods, and the distinction which is made between Jews and Gentiles all indicate that we are again under the Old Testament economy. Chronologically, the seventh trumpet brings us to the return of Christ at the end of the Great Tribulation Period.

DATE FOR THE ENDING OF "THE TIMES OF THE GENTILES"

Here we deal with an indication of projected time periods for the close of the Great Tribulation.

> **And there was given me a reed like unto a rod: and the angel stood, saying, Rise, and measure the temple of God, and the altar, and them that worship therein.**
>
> **But the court which is without the temple leave out, and measure it not; for it is given unto the Gentiles: and the holy city shall they tread under foot forty and two months [Rev. 11:1–2].**

Let me give you my own translation:

> *And there was given me a read like a rod, saying, Rise and measure the temple (holy place) of God, and the altar, and them that worship therein. And the court which is without the temple cast out* [Gr.: *ekbale,* throw out] *and measure it not; for it is given to the nations, and the holy city shall they tread under foot forty and two months.*

We are dealing here with that period that the Lord Jesus spoke of in Luke 21:24, ". . . and Jerusalem shall be trodden down of the Gentiles, until the times of the Gentiles be fulfilled." A great many people thought that when Israel captured Jerusalem, that was the end of the Time of the Gentiles. My friend, Jerusalem is still trodden down of the Gentiles. All you need to do is walk down the streets of the old city, and if you see a Jew, you let me know because I did not see any there myself. All other races are there. Non-Jewish religious groups are all over the place; they have built holy places everywhere in the old city of Jerusalem. Jerusalem is still trodden down of the Gentiles. But when you get into the Great Tribulation Period and come to the last half of it, the Time of the Gentiles will run out in forty-two months. Forty-two months is one-half of the Great Tribulation Period.

"And there was given me a reed like a rod." Every time you see the beginning of measurements, in either the Old or New Testament, it indicates that God is beginning to deal with the nation Israel (see Jer. 31:38–39; Zech. 2). This reed is like a rod; a rod is used by a shepherd. In Psalm 2:9 we see that a rod is used for chastisement and judgment: "Thou shalt break them with a rod of iron; thou shalt dash them in pieces like a potter's vessel." What we are dealing with here is a measurement of time given for the Time of the Gentiles, after which judgment will come upon them. The rod is also for comfort: "Yea, though I walk through the valley of the shadow of death, I will fear no evil: for thou art with me; thy rod and thy staff they comfort me" (Ps. 23:4). Therefore, we have both judgment and solace in this chapter.

"The temple of God" is limited to the Holy Place (notice that "holy place" is the literal rendering) and the Holy of Holies. The temple of God places us back on Old Testament ground, for there is no temple given to the church. The church *is* a temple of the Holy Spirit today; that is, believers (not a building) are the temple of the Holy Spirit: "In whom all the building fitly framed together groweth unto an holy temple in the Lord: In whom ye also are builded together for an habitation of God through the Spirit" (Eph. 2:21–22).

"The altar" refers to the golden altar of prayer since the altar for burnt offering was not in the temple proper but in the outer court.

Even the worshipers are to be measured. John is told to rise and measure, not only the Holy Place and the altar, but also "them that worship therein." God does count the number of those who worship Him.

"And the court which is without the temple cast out [Gr.: *ekbale*, throw out] and measure it not." This excludes all that does not belong to the temple proper. The altar of burnt offering (and also the brazen laver) would be outside the temple. Since this altar was a picture of the cross of Christ, it would seem that the implication is that the gospel of the cross of Christ will still be available to all mankind during the intensity of this brief crisis. It is not be be measured, and it will still be available.

"For it is given to the nations [that is, the Gentiles]" declares that although this period still belongs to the Gentiles, their dominion is limited to forty-two months. As we have said, this confirms the words of the Lord Jesus in Luke 21:24.

"Forty and two months" is the three and one-half year period identified with the last half of the Great Tribulation Period. We find this repeated in Revelation 13:5: "And there was given unto him a mouth speaking great things and blasphemies; and power was given unto him to continue forty and two months." This is the last half of the reign of Antichrist here upon this earth. This period is mentioned again in chapter 12, verse 14: "And to the woman were given two wings of a great eagle, that she might fly into the wildernsess, into her place, where she is nourished for a time, and times, and half a time, from the face of the serpent." "A time, times [dual], and half a time" means three and one-half years.

Daniel adopts this unit of measurement for this period: "And he shall speak great words against the most High, and shall wear out the saints of the most High, and think to change times and laws: and they shall be given into his hand until a time and times and the dividing of time" (Dan. 7:25). "A time and times and the dividing of time"—again, this means three and one-half years. "And from the time that the daily sacrifice shall be taken away, and the abomination that maketh desolate set up, there shall be a thousand two hundred and ninety days" (Dan. 12:11). Twelve hundred and ninety days is three and one-half years. We have yet another reference in Daniel which says: "And he shall confirm the covenant with many for one week: and in the midst of the week he shall cause the sacrifice and the oblation to cease, and for the overspreading of abominations he shall make it desolate, even until the consummation, and that determined shall be poured upon the desolate" (Dan 9:27). Here the Great Tribulation is divided into two equal parts. This "week" of Daniel is seven years, and this seven-year period is the Seventieth Week of Daniel, or the Great Tribulation Period.

DURATION OF THE PROPHESYING OF THE TWO WITNESSES

And I will give power unto my two witnesses, and they shall prophesy a thousand two hundred and threescore days, clothed in sackcloth [Rev. 11:3].

And I will give to my two witnesses, and they shall prophesy a thousand, two hundred and three score [60] days, clothed in sackcloth.

There is a great deal of difference of opinion as to the identity of the two witnesses. They are introduced to us without any suggestion as to who they are. Godet makes this comment: "They are one of the most startling features of the book." If the identity of these two was essential for the understanding of this book, I think there would have been some indication given about their persons. It is always in these areas that the sensational preachers concentrate. They can tell you what the seven thunders said (John was told not to write it down, and he didn't), and they can tell you the names of these two witnesses. Those who have espoused the historical view of Revelation have named such men as John Huss, Pope Sylvester, Waldenson, and the two Testaments. You can see that you could come up with almost anything from that viewpoint. Men who hold the futurist view—which is the view I hold—are not in complete agreement as to who they are. Seiss and Govett say that they are Enoch and Elijah. Govett (*The Apocalypse Expounded by Scripture*, p. 225) says that *The Gospel of Nicodemus* contains the following statement:

> I am Enoch who pleased God, and was translated by him. And this is Elijah the Tishbite. We are also to live to the end of the age: but then we are about to be sent by God to resist Antichrist, and be slain by him, and to rise after three days, and to be caught up in the clouds to meet the Lord.

Dean Alford, Walter Scott, and Donald Grey Barnhouse state that they are Moses and Elijah. William Newell does a very smart thing—he does not even attempt to identify them. There is also the possibility that they are two unknown witnesses—that is, they have had no previous existence, and they have not yet appeared on the scene.

That they are human witnesses seems certain from the description given of them. Two is the required number of witnesses according to the Law: "At the mouth of two witnesses, or three witnesses, shall he that is worthy of death be put to death; but at the mouth of one witness he shall not be put to death" (Deut. 17:6).

The Lord Jesus said the same thing relative to the church: "But if he will not hear thee, then take with thee one or two more, that in the mouth of two or three witnesses every word may be established" (Matt. 18:16). Scripture has always required two witnesses to bear testimony to anything before it was to be heard. Therefore, we can definitely say that these witnesses are human beings and that there are two of them. These are the two things we know for sure.

It seems to me to be almost certain that Elijah is one of them, since it was predicted that he would return: "Behold, I will send you Elijah the prophet before the coming of the great and dreadful day of the

LORD" (Mal. 4:5). It is also recorded in Matthew's Gospel: "And Jesus answered and said unto them, Elias truly shall first come, and restore all things" (Matt. 17:11). It would seem that we can say with a certain degree of assurance that Elijah is one of the witnesses. It is said in verse 4 that these two witnesses are two lampstands standing before "the God of the earth." This was a favorite expression of Elijah who walked out onto the pages of Scripture, saying, ". . . As the LORD God of Israel liveth, before whom I stand . . ." (1 Kings 17:1). These witnesses are two lampstands; they are lights in the world. The presence of Elijah on the Mount of Transfiguration further suggests this, but it would necessitate the second witness being Moses, which is more difficult to sustain, and after all, the Mount of Transfiguration is not the only point of similarity.

I would like to make a suggestion about which I will not be dogmatic nor will I argue. My suggestion is that John the Baptist is the second witness. He was the forerunner of Christ at His first coming. He was similar to Elijah in manner and message. I am sure that those two fellows would get along with each other. Both knew what it was to oppose the forces of darkness and to stand alone for God against impossible odds. They surely have had good training in the past. John the Baptist would be the witness of the New Testament, as Elijah would be the witness of the Old Testament. John the Baptist actually was not part of the church, the bride of Christ. He very candidly said that he was a friend of the Bridegroom. He wasn't a bride; he was a friend of the Bridegroom.

It seems unlikely that Enoch would be one of the witnesses since he was a Gentile. The very fact that he did not die does not qualify him for the office for, by the time you come to the Great Tribulation Period, the church has already been translated, and some of them were translated without dying.

Let us say with some assurance that Elijah is one of the witnesses. As to who the other one is, your guess is as good as mine.

"And they shall prophecy a thousand, two hundred and threescore days." The significant feature about the two witnesses is not their identity but the time they appear. Is this during the first half or the last half of the Great Tribulation? The first half seems to fit the text more accurately because they testify until the Beast appears, and then they are martyred.

"Clothed in sackcloth" is the garb better suited to the period of the Law than of grace. It is becoming both to Elijah and to John the Baptist.

> **These are the two olive trees, and the two candlesticks standing before the God of the earth.**
>
> **And if any man will hurt them, fire proceedeth out of their mouth, and devoureth their enemies: and if any man will hurt them, he must in this manner be killed [Rev. 11:4–5].**
>
> *These are the two olive trees and the two lampstands standing before the Lord of the earth. And if anyone wishes to hurt them, fire proceedeth out of their mouth and devoureth their enemies; and if anyone wishes to hurt them, thus must he be killed.*

Everything here is associated with the Old Testament. The two olive trees immediately suggest the vision in Zechariah 4. There the lampstands are two individuals, Joshua and Zerubbabel, who were enabled by the Holy Spirit to stand against insurmountable difficulties. The explanation is found in the words, ". . . Not by might, nor by power [or, not by brain, nor by brawn], but by my spirit, saith the LORD of hosts" (Zech. 4:6). The Holy Spirit will be present during the Great Tribulation Period.

These two witnesses are lights before the powers of darkness. These men are accorded miraculous power to bring fire down from heaven—they are filled with the Holy Spirit. Here again, the suggestion is strongly in favor of Elijah (see 1 Kings 18:38; 2 Kings 1:10). Also, John made an announcement about One baptizing with fire (see Matt. 3:11).

These two witnesses are immortal and immune to all attacks until their mission is completed. My friend, it is encouraging to know that all of God's men are immortal until He has accomplished His purpose through them. This is one reason that I have had a weak and feeble faith through several cancer surgeries and other physical problems. I will be honest with you, there were times when I wondered if I would make it through or not. But I prayed to God and asked other people to pray that I might be enabled to finish the taping of our five-year "Thru the Bible" radio broadcasts—and He has answered that prayer. That all of God's men are immortal until God is through with them is a wonderful comforting thought for today. And when He is through with you, He will remove you from the earth.

> **These have power to shut heaven, that it rain not in the days of their prophecy: and have power over waters to turn them to blood, and to smite the earth with all plagues, as often as they will [Rev. 11:6].**
>
> *These have the authority* [Gr.: *exousian*—power] *to shut up the heaven, that the rain may not wet during the days of their prophecy; and they have power over the waters to turn them into blood, and to smite the earth with every plague, as often as they wish.*

These two witnesses are granted unlimited authority. They control rainfall on the earth, and they are able to turn the water into blood. This certainly reminds us of both Elijah and Moses. This is the verse that has caused certain outstanding men to decide that Elijah, who was the man that stopped the rain, and Moses, who was the one who brought the plagues upon Egypt, will be the two. They may have good ground for that, but anything you say about these two witnesses is speculation.

"And to smite the earth"—they are given the same power Christ will have when He returns (see Rev. 19:15).

"With every plague" suggests the plagues Moses imposed on Egypt, but the plagues here are greater in number as the territory is more vast.

"As often as they wish" reveals the confidence God places in these faithful servants. God cannot trust you and me like this. He cannot trust some of us with money; certainly He wasn't able to trust me with very much. He does not trust us with power, and this is the reason that He removes men from office after a period of time—time is always on His side—because He cannot trust men with power. It is a good thing that many of us do not have it.

> **And when they shall have finished their testimony, the beast that ascendeth out of the bottomless pit shall make war against them, and shall overcome them, and kill them [Rev. 11:7].**
>
> *And when they shall have finished their testimony, the wild beast that cometh up out of the abyss, shall make war with them, and overcome them, and kill them.*

The witnesses will finish their testimony. In the midst of the week, the Antichrist, who is the Beast, the Man of Sin who is moving to power, will bring back first the Roman Empire. Then, when he gets the whole world under his control, he will not hesitate to overcome and destroy these two witnesses. At that time he will be permitted to do so. This is the temporary victory of darkness over light, evil over righteousness, hell over heaven, and Satan over God, because God is going to let Satan loose during this period.

These witnesses live up to their name. *Martus* is the Greek word for "witness"; we get our English word *martyr* from that.

> **And their dead bodies shall lie in the street of the great city, which spiritually is called Sodom and Egypt, where also our Lord was crucified [Rev. 11:8].**
>
> *And their dead bodies (carcasses) shall lie upon the street of the great city, which spiritually is called Sodom and Egypt, where also their Lord was crucified.*

These men are not given even a decent burial. This reveals the crude, cold barbarism of the last days which will be covered with but a thin veneer of culture. There is a strange resemblance to the sadistic curiosity which placed two dead men, Lenin and Stalin, on display in Red Square in Moscow. They have removed Stalin, but at this writing Lenin is still there, and I understand that that body is beginning to deteriorate.

The word used for *bodies* (carcasses) denotes the contempt and hatred the world will have for the two witnesses. They are treated as dead animals.

"The great city" is Jerusalem. It is likened unto Sodom by Isaiah (see Isa. 1:10). It is called Egypt because the world has entered into every fiber of its life—social and political. It is conclusively identified as Jerusalem by the sad designation, "where also their Lord was crucified."

And they of the people and kindreds and tongues and nations shall see their dead bodies three days and a half, and shall not suffer their dead bodies to be put in graves [Rev. 11:9].

And out of the peoples, and tribes, and tongues, and nations do some gaze upon their dead bodies (carcasses) three days and one half and shall not permit their dead bodies (carcasses) to be put in a tomb.

After Christ was crucified, even Pilate permitted His friends to take down the body and give it a respectable burial, but not so with the two witnesses. The world will be startled to hear they are dead. Some will be skeptical. Apparently, this future generation will have something that corresponds to a television camera, and a satellite will carry the picture all over the world, so that people everywhere will be able to look upon the features of these men for three and one-half days. The morbid curiosity of a godless society will relish the opportunity of gazing with awe upon these dead bodies. This is the worst indignity that a depraved world could vent upon the men who denounced them and their wicked ways. Perhaps the witnesses had predicted their resurrection. We are not told that, but they might have. To prevent the possibility of another empty tomb, there was no burial. They will decide to just leave the bodies out there and keep the camera on them. I think all the television networks will have their cameras trained on these dead men. Three and one-half days they are lying there.

> **And they that dwell upon the earth shall rejoice over them, and make merry, and shall send gifts one to another; because these two prophets tormented them that dwelt on the earth [Rev. 11:10].**
>
> *And the dwellers upon the earth rejoice over them, and make merry, and shall send gifts one to another; because these two prophets tormented (vexed) the dwellers on the earth.*

The death of the two witnesses is an occasion for high carnival on the earth. The world engages in a modern Christmas and Mardi Gras, both rolled into one. The world has adopted the philosophy, "Let us eat, drink, and be merry, for tomorrow we die." Dr. Newell describes it like this: "Now comes the real revelation of the heart of man: glee, horrid, insane, inhuman, hellish, ghoulish glee!"

"And shall send gifts one to another" indicates a lovely occasion on the surface, but this is the Devil's Christmas. The modern celebration of Christmas gets farther and farther from the birth of Christ and closer and closer to paganism. The day will come when it will be anti-Christian—it is almost that now. Here is the celebration of what Antichrist has done instead of the celebration of the coming of Christ to Bethlehem.

Then something happens—

> **And after three days and an half the Spirit of life from God entered into them, and they stood upon their feet; and great fear fell upon them which saw them [Rev. 11:11].**
>
> *And after the three days and a half the breath (spirit) of life from God entered into them, and they stood upon*

their feet; and great fear fell upon them that beheld them.

While the world is celebrating in jubilation the death of these witnesses and while the television cameras are focused upon them, the witnesses will stand on their feet. And all of the networks will regret that they had their cameras pointed to them, because they will not really want to give the news as it is. The scriptural word for resurrection is used here—the Greek word *histeme*—"they stood upon their feet." These witnesses are among the Tribulation saints who have part in the first resurrection (see Rev. 20:4–6). Any news like this would be a scoop, but I am sure that all of the networks will have their cameras on it. By that time they may well have some new gadget which will make television, as we know it, look very much antiquated and out of place.

And they heard a great voice from heaven saying unto them, Come up hither. And they ascended up to heaven in a cloud; and their enemies beheld them [Rev. 11:12].

And they heard a great voice out of heaven saying to them, Come up here, and they went up into heaven in the cloud, and their enemies beheld them.

They are caught up into heaven. We have the *resurrection* of the two witnesses in verse 11; we have the *ascension* of the two witnesses in verse 12. The cloud of glory is associated with the ascension and the coming of Christ also.

DOOM OF THE SECOND WOE—GREAT EARTHQUAKE

We have had the blowing of the sixth trumpet, and we are in that interval or lull between the sixth and seventh trumpets. These are woe trumpets, and the second woe is connected with the sixth trumpet—it is a great earthquake.

And the same hour was there a great earthquake, and the tenth part of the city fell, and in the earthquake were slain of men seven thousand: and the remnant were affrighted, and gave glory to the God of heaven [Rev. 11:13].

And in that hour there came to pass a great earthquake, and a tenth of the city fell, and 7000 names of men were killed in the earthquake, and the rest were afraid, and gave glory to the God of heaven.

This number of the slain was to be added to those already slain. A fourth of the population of the world was slain at first, and then a third of the population of the world—totaling over one-half—and now seven thousand more are killed. It is little wonder that the Lord Jesus said, "And except those days should be shortened, there should no flesh be saved . . ." (Matt. 24:22).

The earthquake seems to be limited to the city of Jerusalem, just as it was when Christ rose from the dead (see Matt. 28:2), and also at His crucifixion (see Matt. 27:51–52).

"Seven thousand names of men were killed in the earthquake." This is an idiom to indicate that they were men of prominence. They were the ones who had gone along with Antichrist, men whose names got into the headlines when Antichrist came to power.

The second woe is past; and, behold, the third woe cometh quickly [Rev. 11:14].

This ends the second woe. The third woe begins shortly, though not immediately. The third woe is not the blowing of the seventh trumpet which will come next, as that leads us beyond the Great Tribulation into the Millennium. The seventh trumpet likewise opens up to us the seven personalities of chapters 12 and 13. The third woe begins when Satan, one of the personalities, is cast down to earth, and we will come to that in chapter 12, verse 12.

SEVENTH TRUMPET—END OF GREAT TRIBULATION AND OPENING OF TEMPLE IN HEAVEN

In the middle of all the woes and judgments of the Great Tribulation Period, this is inserted for the encouragement of the believers who will be left on the earth, those who were sealed. They are apt to get very much discouraged after several years, although the total length of the Great Tribulation is but seven years and the intensity of it breaks in the last half of that period. The Great Tribulation does not seem long to read about, but I have found seven *days* in the hospital to be the most trying experience of life. I thought those days would never end; so you do need a little encouragement as you go along.

> **And the seventh angel sounded; and there were great voices in heaven, saying, The kingdoms of this world are become the kingdoms of our Lord, and of his Christ; and he shall reign for ever and ever.**
>
> **And the four and twenty elders, which sat before God on their seats, fell upon their faces, and worshipped God,**
>
> **Saying, We give thee thanks, O Lord God Almighty, which art, and wast, and art to come; because thou hast taken to thee thy great power, and hast reigned.**
>
> **And the nations were angry, and thy wrath is come, and the time of the dead, that they should be judged, and that thou shouldest give reward unto thy servants the prophets, and to the saints, and them that fear thy name, small and great; and shouldest destroy them which destroy the earth [Rev. 11:15–18].**

> *And the seventh angel blew the trumpet; and there followed (came to pass) great voices in heaven, saying, The kingdom of the world (cosmos) is become (the kingdom) of our Lord, and of His Christ; and He shall reign unto*

> *the ages of the ages (for ever and ever). And the twenty-four elders, sitting before God on their thrones, fell upon their faces, and worshipped God, saying, We give thanks to you, O Lord God the Almighty, who art and who wast; because thou hast taken thy great power and didst reign. And the nations were angry (wroth), and thy wrath came, and the time (period) of the dead to be judged, and to give the reward to your servants the prophets and to the saints and to them that fear thy name, the small and great; and to destroy those who destroy (corrupt, the destroyers of) the earth.*

The blowing of the seventh trumpet is of utmost significance, and it is of special relevance in the understanding of the remainder of this book. In the program of God, it brings us chronologically to the breathtaking entrance of eternity where the mystery of God is finally unraveled. It brings us in God's program as far as chapter 21 where eternity begins. The broad outline of events which are significant to God is given to us here by the Holy Spirit. This section is a summary, a syllabus, or a capsule synopsis of events up to the door of eternity. The following list will help focus these events in our minds:

1. "Great voices in heaven" follow the blowing of the seventh trumpet. At the opening of the seventh seal, there was silence in heaven. The contrast should be noted, because here the blowing of the seventh trumpet reveals God's program and clears up the mystery of God. All of God's created intelligences can see the end now and are jubilant in anticipation of the termination of evil being so close at hand. It is a time of joy for them.

2. "The kingdom of the world (cosmos) is become (the kingdom) of our Lord, and of His Christ; and He shall reign unto the ages of the ages (for ever and ever)." It is not kingdoms (plural) but kingdom (singular) which denotes the fact that the kingdoms of this world are at present under Satan, to whom there is no distinction of nations, no East or West, no Iron Curtain—all are his; both sides are included in his domain. A great many people think that Satan is controlling Russia but that the Lord is controlling the United States and angels are

hovering over the capitol at Washington, D.C. May I say that those angels may not be God's angels who are hovering over Washington today—it certainly doesn't look like they are. Actually, *all* of the kingdoms of this world are Satan's. It is therefore called the kingdom—not kingdoms—of the world. It is the totality of a civilization and society of which men boast of self-improvement but which becomes more godless and wicked each day. It is a condemned civilization that is moving toward judgment.

It is going to become the kingdom "of our Lord, and of His Christ." Satan's kingdom is going to be subdued someday, but not by some little saccharine-sweet talk on brotherhood and love. It is going to be delivered to the Lord Jesus Christ, and He is going to rule. We are told in Scripture: "The kings of the earth set themselves, and the rulers take counsel together, against the LORD, and against his anointed, saying, Let us break their bands asunder, and cast away their cords from us" (Ps. 2:2–3). Rebellion broke out against the Lord and His Christ (Messiah, Anointed) at the arrest of Jesus. The early church understood that this was the condition of the world, for they quoted Psalm 2 when persecution broke out in the early church (see Acts 4:23–26). We read in Psalm 2:9: "Thou shalt break them with a rod of iron; thou shalt dash them in pieces like a potter's vessel." In Revelation 19 we are going to see the details of what is given here in this section. The Lord Jesus is coming to put down rebellion. The seventh trumpet is moving along, step by step, toward eternity.

3. "And the twenty-four elders, sitting before God on their thrones, fell upon their faces, and worshipped God, saying, We give thanks to you, O Lord God the Alnighty, who art and who wast; because thou hast taken thy great power and didst reign." This revelation causes the church in heaven to worship and celebrate the coming of Christ to the earth. This will be the answer to our prayer, "Thy kingdom come. Thy will be done in earth, as it is in heaven" (Matt. 6:10).

4. "The nations were angry (wroth)" reveals the fact that the stubborn rebellion of man will continue right down to the very end. Right down to the wire, the stubborn heart of man is in rebellion against God. This old nature, this carnal nature that you and I have, is

not obedient to God. My friend, you cannot make this old nature obey God. This is exactly what Paul says: "Because the carnal mind is enmity against God: for it is not subject to the law of God, neither indeed can be" (Rom. 8:7). The human family could not bring this old nature under control; that is the reason God is going to get rid of it someday.

5. The nations were angry because "thy wrath came." They had been fed all this putrid pabulum we hear today about the fact that God never intends to punish sin and that man is getting better and better every day—while, actually, all the time he is getting worse and worse.

6. "And the time (period) of the dead to be judged" brings us to the Great White Throne judgment of the lost dead (see Rev. 20:11–15).

7. "And to give the reward to your servants the prophets and to the saints and to them that fear thy name, the small and great." The church has already gone into His presence, and the believers there have already been rewarded as indicated by the crowns we have seen on the heads of the elders. This refers now to Old Testament saints and Tribulation saints, who are included in the first resurrection, but at a different time. They are now going to be rewarded as the kingdom begins.

8. "And to destroy those who destroy (corrupt, the destroyers of) the earth." We believe that this refers to both man and Satan. Man is a destroyer as well as Satan. Peter warns us of Satan: "Be sober, be vigilant; because your adversary the devil, as a roaring lion, walketh about, seeking whom he may devour" (1 Pet. 5:8).

The next verse brings us to the glad gate of eternity:

> **And the temple of God was opened in heaven, and there was seen in his temple the ark of his testament: and there were lightnings, and voices, and thunderings, and an earthquake, and great hail [Rev. 11:19].**

> *And the sanctuary (temple) of God in heaven was opened, and the ark of His covenant was seen in His sanctuary (temple), and there followed lightnings, and voices, and thunders, and an earthquake, and great hail.*

When we see the church again, it will be in the New Jerusalem, and we are told definitely that there is no temple there. Here there is a temple in heaven. The temple which Moses made was made after the pattern in heaven. "And the sanctuary (temple) of God in heaven was opened" means that God is dealing now with Israel.

"Was opened" indicates worship and access to God. All of this points to the nation Israel, for the church has no temple. The measuring of the temple on earth and the opening of the temple in heaven declare the prominence of Israel in this section. The next chapter will substantiate this.

"And the ark of His covenant was seen in His sanctuary (temple)" reminds us that we are dealing with a covenant-making and covenant-keeping God. He is going to keep the covenant He has made with Israel, and He will make a New Covenant with them at this time—that is, the Law will be written in their hearts instead of on cold tablets of stone (see Jer. 31:31–34; Heb. 8:8–13).

"Lightnings, and voices, and thunders, and an earthquake, and great hail" speak of judgment yet to come.

CHAPTER 12

***THEME:** Seven performers during the Great Tribulation*

The theme of this chapter is the final conflict between Israel and Satan after he is cast out of heaven. Seven performers are introduced to us (see chs. 12—13) by the blowing of this seventh trumpet during the Great Tribulation Period. Although the seventh trumpet brings us through the Great Tribulation and the Millennium to the very threshold of eternity, a great deal was omitted. Beginning with chapter 12, this will be compensated for in the presentation of seven prominent personages who play a dominant part in the Great Tribulation Period. After that, we will have the pouring out of the seven bowls of wrath and then the final destruction of commercial Babylon and religious Babylon.

The prominence of the nation Israel is brought before us. It was suggested in the previous chapter with the measuring of the temple on earth and the opening of the temple in heaven. The last verse of chapter 11 is actually the opening to this chapter.

These seven personages are representatives of persons, both natural and supernatural, physical and spiritual, rulers and nations. The identification and clarification of these are essential for a proper understanding of the Revelation.

THE WOMAN—ISRAEL

As we take up the very first one of these personalities, it will illustrate this point. We come now to the crux of the interpretation of the entire Book of Revelation which revolves about this first personality. An outstanding and very intellectual minister years ago made the statement: "If you tell me your interpretation of the woman in the twelfth chapter of Revelation, then I'll tell you your interpretation of prophecy." At the time, I thought he was foolish, but I have come to agree with him. I believe that the identification of this woman is the key to the understanding of the Book of Revelation.

> **And there appeared a great wonder in heaven; a woman clothed with the sun, and the moon under her feet, and upon her head a crown of twelve stars:**
>
> **And she being with child cried, travailing in birth, and pained to be delivered [Rev. 12:1–2].**

Let me give you my translation:

> *And a great sign was seen in heaven: a woman arrayed with the sun, and the moon under her feet, and upon her head a crown of twelve stars; and she was with child, and travailing in birth, and being tormented to be delivered.*

The important thing here is: "Who is the woman?" You are acquainted with the interpretation of the Roman church that she represents the Virgin Mary. There are Protestant interpreters who have been as far wrong as that. Today most of them follow the method of Rome and interpret the woman as the church of all ages. Practically all denominational literature follows this line.

There have been several female founders of cults who could not resist the temptation of seeing themselves pictured in this woman. Joanna Southcott said that she herself was the woman in chapter 12 and that in October, 1814, she would have the man child. She never did, but she had 200,000 followers. We have had in the United States several founders of cults and religions who thought they were this woman. In Southern California, we even had a few female preachers who got the idea they might be the woman, but they weren't. We can dismiss all these claims, unless we want to forsake all intelligent approach to the interpretation of Scripture.

The identifying marks of the woman are the sun, moon, and stars.

These belong to Israel as seen in Joseph's dream: "And he dreamed yet another dream, and told it his brethren, and said, Behold, I have dreamed a dream more; and, behold, the sun and the moon and the eleven stars made obeisance to me. And he told it to his father, and to his brethren: and his father rebuked him, and said unto him, What is this dream that thou hast dreamed? Shall I and thy mother and thy brethren indeed come to bow down ourselves to thee to the earth?" (Gen. 37:9–10). Old Jacob interpreted the sun, moon, and stars to mean himself, Rachel, and Joseph's brothers. And they did bow down before Joseph before things were over with (although Rachel had died by that time).

The woman is a sign in heaven, although her career is here in earth. She is not a literal woman; she is a symbol. The career of the woman corresponds to that of Israel, for it is Israel that gave birth to Christ, who is the Child.

At Christmastime we all use Isaiah 9:6 and other verses concerning the birth of Christ. This verse does concern the birth of Christ, but it does not concern us at all; rather, it concerns the nation Israel. "For unto us a child is born, unto us a son is given: and the government shall be upon his shoulder: and his name shall be called Wonderful, Counsellor, The mighty God, The everlasting Father, The Prince of Peace" (Isa. 9:6). Who is referred to here when Isaiah says, "Unto us"? The church? No; it's the nation Israel. It is quite obvious that Isaiah is speaking to the nation Israel, and he is speaking not relative to a Savior but to a Governor, a Ruler, a King, One who was to come and rule over them. "For unto us a child is born, unto us a son is given." It is interesting that as a child He was *born* in His humanity; but as a Son from eternity, He was *given*. "And the government shall be upon his shoulder"—we are not talking now about the Savior but about the One who is coming as King. We will see that happen in the Book of Revelation. "And his name shall be called Wonderful, Counsellor, The mighty God, The everlasting Father, The Prince of Peace." There will not be any peace until He comes. When the rulers of this world say, ". . . Peace and safety; then sudden destruction cometh upon them . . ." (1 Thess. 5:3). They were having a big peace conference in Holland when World War I broke out, and most of the delegates almost got fired upon before they got home! When men say, "Peace and safety," it is idle talk, because man is working at peace from the wrong end. It is the human heart that is wrong, and only Jesus will bring peace. He is the Prince of Peace. Isaiah is talking to Israel when he says, "Unto us a child is born," and that is the figure that John picks up here in Revelation.

The writer to the Hebrews says, "For it is evident that our Lord sprang out of Juda . . ." (Heb. 7:14). Paul writes in Romans: "Who are Israelites; to whom pertaineth the adoption, and the glory, and the covenants, and the giving of the law, and the service of God, and the promises; whose are the fathers, and of whom as concerning the flesh Christ came, who is over all, God blessed for ever. Amen" (Rom. 9:4–5). Paul is talking about Israel. He begins by asking the question: "Who are Israelites?" The answer just happens to be: "And of whom as concerning the flesh Christ came." The woman at the well was accurate when she identified the Lord Jesus as a Jew: ". . . How is it that thou, being a *Jew*, askest drink of me, which am a woman of Samaria? . . ." (John 4:9, italics mine). We read in Micah 5:2–3: "But thou, Bethlehem Ephratah, though thou be little among the thousands of Judah, yet out of thee shall he come forth unto me that is to be ruler of Israel; whose goings forth have been from of old, from everlasting. Therefore will he give them up, until the time that she which travaileth hath brought forth: then the remnant of his brethren shall return unto the children of Israel." Notice that He will be born in Bethlehem, but He comes out of eternity.

"Travailing in birth" is a figure associated with Israel: "Before she travailed, she brought forth; before her pain came, she was delivered of a man child. Who hath heard such a thing? who hath seen such things? Shall the earth be made to bring forth in one day? or shall a nation be born at once? for as soon as Zion travailed, she brought forth her children" (Isa. 66:7–8). Israel will go through the Great Tribulation after Christ was born in Bethlehem—"before her pain came, she was delivered of a man child," meaning Christ.

Therefore, we identify the woman as the nation Israel. No one woman who has ever lived, including the Virgin Mary, fits into this. It is the nation Israel and certainly not the church of all ages. If we just keep our bearings here and not lose our heads, we know that this is the Great Tribulation Period and that the church has already gone to heaven. This woman is not the church of all ages.

"Being tormented." Certainly Israel has suffered satanic anti-Semitism from the time of the birth of Christ to the present, in fact, even since before that day, because Satan knew that Christ would come from this nation.

THE RED DRAGON—SATAN

We now have introduced to us another character, and this character is really not a delightful one at all. This is the red dragon. This is not a comic-strip characterization, for there is nothing funny about him. This is very solemn and serious.

> **And there appeared another wonder in heaven; and behold a great red dragon, having seven heads and ten horns, and seven crowns upon his heads.**
>
> **And his tail drew the third part of the stars of heaven, and did cast them to the earth: and the dragon stood before the woman which was ready to be delivered, for to devour her child as soon as it was born [Rev. 12:3–4].**
>
> *And there was seen another sign in heaven, and behold, a great red dragon having seven heads and ten horns and on his head seven diadems (kingly crowns). And his tail draweth the third of the stars of heaven, and he did cast [aorist tense] them into the earth. And the dragon stood before the woman about to be delivered, that when she was delivered he might devour her child.*

"And there was seen another sign in heaven." Notice that these are *signs* that are given to us; they are not literal. I told you that if John is giving you a symbol, he will make it clear that it is a symbol.

The red dragon is clearly identified as Satan in verse 9: "And the great dragon was cast out, that old serpent, called the Devil, and Satan, which deceiveth the whole world: he was cast out into the earth, and his angels were cast out with him." We can identify this character without speculating at all.

In this second sign, the true character of Satan is revealed with all the wrappings removed:

1. He is called "great" because of his vast power. He controls the nations of the world and offered them to the Lord Jesus if He would worship him (see Matt. 4:8–9). Worship of himself is Satan's ultimate goal. The kingdoms of this world are his, and he controls them today. In that day it was Rome, but he has controlled every nation.

2. He is called "red" because of the fact that he was a murderer from the beginning (see John 8:44). He has no regard for human life. I do not understand why so many serve him. Why is it that alcohol finally kills its victims? It is the worst killer there is today. It is because Satan is back of it, my friend, and he has no regard for human life at all.

3. He is called a "dragon" because of the viciousness of his character. He was originally created Lucifer, son of the morning (see Ezek. 28:12–19), but he is now the epitome of evil and the depth of degradation. He is the most dangerous being in all of God's creation. He is my enemy, and he is your enemy if you are a child of God.

The reason that the Beast in chapter 13 is similar to the dragon is because both the restored Roman Empire and Antichrist are empowered and controlled by Satan. Rome, through the instrumentality of both Herod and Pilate, sought to destroy the child of the woman.

"Seven heads" suggests the perfection of wisdom which characterized the creation of Satan who was originally the "covering cherub." Ezekiel 28:12 speaks of how he was at his origin: ". . . full of wisdom, and perfect in beauty." This reveals two of the fallacies that the world has concerning Satan. This world thinks he is ugly, but may I say to you, he was created "perfect in beauty." If you could see him, you would not see the foul creature that is often pictured for us by the world. Sometimes he is pictured as having horns, cloven feet, and a forked tail. That is the "great god" Pan that the Greeks and Romans worshiped. That is not Satan, although Satan is back of that worship, also. I have seen the ruins of the temple at Pergamum and of other temples to Pan in at least a dozen cities. It is not strange that men are worshiping him; when they will not have God, they certainly will take him. But Satan is smart, he's clever, and he's wise. You and I are no match for him at all. We will be overcome if we try to stand in our own strength against him. He is not only beautiful, he is also full of wisdom. This is the way he is presented in Scripture.

"Ten horns" suggests the final division of the Roman Empire, which is dominated by Satan and which is his final effort to rule the world. The crowns are on the horns, not on the heads, since it is delegated power from Satan. The crowns represent kingly authority and rulership.

"The third of the stars of heaven" indicates the vast extent of the rebellion in heaven when one third of the angelic host followed Satan to their own destruction. Daniel makes reference to this in an admittedly difficult passage (see Dan. 8:10; Jude 6).

The dragon hates the Man Child because it was predicted from the beginning that the child would be the undoing of Satan. "And I will put enmity between thee and the woman, and between thy seed and her seed; it shalt bruise thy head, and thou shalt bruise his heel" (Gen. 3:15).

THE CHILD OF THE WOMAN—JESUS CHRIST

And she brought forth a man child, who was to rule all nations with a rod of iron: and her child was caught up unto God, and to his throne.

And the woman fled into the wilderness, where she hath a place prepared of God, that they should feed her there a thousand two hundred and threescore days [Rev. 12:5–6].

And she was delivered of a son, a man child, who is to shepherd (rule) all the nations with a rod of iron, and her child was caught up unto God and His throne. And the woman fled into the wilderness, where she hath a place prepared of (from) God, that there they may nourish her a thousand two hundred and sixty (1260) days.

The "man child" is Christ. He is easily identified here. I hope that you will not fall into the error of equating the Child with the church, although many have done that.

"Who is to shepherd (rule) all the nations with a rod of iron" is a clear-cut reference to Christ. "Thou shalt break them with a rod of iron; thou shalt dash them in pieces like a potter's vessel" (Ps. 2:9). In Acts 4 the persecuted Christians quoted Psalm 2, identifying the One to rule with a rod of iron as the Lord Jesus Christ.

Christ will come to put down all enmity, all opposition, all rebellion on the earth. How will He do it? He will break them with a rod of iron and dash them in pieces like a potter's vessel. If this peace crowd would only come up with a plan that would not work, it would not be necessary to put down rebellion with a bit of violence. But there is no other way to put it down. How do you think Jesus Christ is going to come to power in a rebellious world? Suppose He was suddenly to appear at the capital of any nation in the world. Do you think they are prepared to surrender to Him and turn all authority over to Him? This includes my own country. Is the United States prepared to yield to Jesus Christ? If you say "Yes," I will have to ask, "Why don't they?" They *could* yield to Him today. My friend, the world is in rebellion against Him. Maybe you are one of the peace crowd. You don't like the shedding of blood, you just hate violence and war—don't we all?—but this is the only way that rebellion can be put down. The Lord Jesus Christ is going to rule.

"And her child was caught up unto God and His throne." This is a reference to the ascension of Christ. In the Gospels the emphasis is on the death of Christ. In the Epistles the emphasis is upon the resurrection of Christ. In the Book of Revelation the emphasis is upon the ascension of Christ. Protestantism, and even fundamentalism, has ignored the ascension of Christ, and this is one reason we have not had a great enough emphasis upon the present ministry of Christ. "And when he had spoken these things, while they beheld, he was taken up; and a cloud received him out of their sight. And while they looked stedfastly toward heaven as he went up, behold, two men stood by them in white apparel; which also said, Ye men of Galilee, why stand ye gazing up into heaven? this same Jesus, which is taken up from you into heaven, shall so come in like manner as ye have seen him go into heaven" (Acts 1:9–11).

The Book of Revelation is the unveiling of the ascended Christ, the glorified Christ, the Christ who is coming in glory. The Book of the Revelation rests upon the fact of the Ascension. He is the One who has been opening the seals which have brought to pass everything that has happened since then. We are told in Hebrews 12:2: "Looking unto Jesus the author and finisher of our faith; who for the joy that was set before him endured the cross, despising the shame, and is set down at the right hand of the throne of God." A great many have the impression that this means He is twiddling His thumbs, but that is because they do not know Revelation. He is not sitting up there doing nothing. He is going to do a great deal because of His ascension into heaven, and He has a present ministry today with the church.

"And she was delivered of a son, a man child." I believe this settles the identity of the woman. Israel is clearly the one from whom Christ came. While the church came from Jesus Christ, He, according to the flesh, came from Israel. Again let me quote Paul: "Who are Israelites . . . of whom as concerning the flesh of Christ came . . ." (Rom. 9:4–5). We are told in Galatians 4:4–5: "But when the fulness of the time was come, God sent forth his Son, made of a woman, made under the law, to redeem them that were under the law, that we might receive the adoption of sons." "Made under the law"—what law? It is the Mosaic Law which was given to Israel. He came "made [or, born] under the law" because He was an Israelite. Again in Galatians we read: "Now to Abraham and his seed were the promises made. He saith not, And to seeds, as of many; but as of one, and to thy seed, which is Christ" (Gal. 3:16). Before the nation came into existence, God said to Abraham, "I am going to make you a great nation, and through that nation I am sending a seed"—not many, but one, and that One is Christ. We have already looked at Isaiah 9:6 which says, "For unto us a child is born, unto us a son is given. . . ." "Us" does not mean the United States, although some seem to think so! "Unto us" means Israel. Isaiah was an Israelite and was speaking to that nation. He was not speaking either to the church or to the Gentiles, but to Israel.

"And the woman fled into the wilderness, where she hath a place prepared of (from) God." During the intense part of the Great Tribulation Period, this remnant of Israel will be protected by God. There are those who dogmatically say that Israel will go to the rock-hewn city of Petra and will be preserved there because no enemy can get in. But in our day an enemy now comes from above and drops down bombs. The last place I would want to be when bombs start falling is within that rock-hewn city of Petra. To make that dogmatic statement alongside clear-cut prophecies is certainly to deceive people. This is not a clear-cut prophecy, and I do not know where the place will be. It does not hurt us preachers to say we don't know something when we don't know. To my judgment it is tragic to be so dogmatic about that which is not revealed. If you want to make such a statement about a speculative Scripture, I will not object if you will say, "This is my judgment," or "I think this is the way it will be."

MICHAEL, THE ARCHANGEL, WARS WITH THE DRAGON

And there was war in heaven: Michael and his angels fought against the dragon; and the dragon fought and his angels,

And prevailed not; neither was their place found any more in heaven.

And the great dragon was cast out, that old serpent, called the Devil, and Satan, which deceiveth the whole world: he was cast out into the earth, and his angels were cast out with him [Rev. 12:7–9].

And there arose war in heaven, Michael and his angels going forth to war with the dragon. And the dragon warred and his angels, and they prevailed not, neither was their place found any more in heaven. And the great dragon was cast down, the old serpent, the one called (the) Devil, and the Satan, he that deceiveth the whole (inhabited) world; he was cast down to the earth, and his angels with him were cast down.

We have here a startling revelation: "And there arose war in heaven." The United Nations could not do anything about this war any more than they could about any other war that has taken place since they came into existence. It is difficult to imagine that there is war in heaven, but Satan still has access to heaven and, as long as he does, there will be this problem.

We are told in the Book of Job that Satan came with the sons of God to appear before God (see Job 1—2). He apparently had as much right there as they did. He had been created the highest creation. We also read in Zechariah 3:1–2: "And he shewed me Joshua the high priest standing before the angel of the LORD, and Satan standing at his right hand to resist him. And the LORD said unto Satan, the LORD rebuke thee, O Satan; even the LORD that hath chosen Jerusalem rebuke thee: is not this a brand plucked out of the fire?" Satan has access to God, and he is able to carry on a communication with God. Luke 22:31 tells us: "And the Lord said, Simon, Simon, behold, Satan hath desired to have you, that he may sift you as wheat." I do not think that Satan sent a Western Union telegram to God or that he telephoned Him. He was able to come into the presence of God, and he requested that he might test this man Simon Peter—and he was granted that permission.

"Michael" is the archangel. We are told this in the Book of Jude: "Yet Michael the archangel, when contending with the devil he disputed about the body of Moses, durst not bring against him a railing accusation, but said, The Lord rebuke thee" (Jude 9). Evidently there are other archangels, but Michael has a peculiar ministry with the nation Israel. Daniel 10:13 tells us: "But the prince of the kingdom of Persia withstood me one and twenty days: but, lo, Michael, one of the chief princes, came to help me; and I remained there with the kings of Persia." Michael is "one of the chief princes." Although there are probably other archangels, Michael and Gabriel are the only ones whose names are given in Scripture. Again in Daniel we read: "But I will shew thee that which is noted in the scripture of truth: and there is none that holdeth with me in these things, but Michael your prince" (Dan. 10:21).

"Michael your prince"—since the Lord is talking to Daniel, this refers to Daniel's people, the nation Israel. This is made clear in Daniel 12:1: "And at that time shall Michael stand up, the great prince which standeth for the children of thy people: and there shall be a time of trouble, such as never was since there was a nation even to that same time: and at that time thy people shall be delivered, every one that shall be found written in the book." At that time, we are told, there will be a time of trouble, the Great Tribulation. Michael will again step out and drive Satan out of heaven, because he happens to be the prince who watches over the nation Israel. This is a tremendous thing, and it beggars description.

There will be a fierce struggle, a war. Satan is not going to retire easily, but Michael and his angels will prevail, and Satan and his angels will be thrown out of heaven. The Lord Jesus referred to this in Luke 10:18, "And he said unto them, I beheld Satan as lightning fall from heaven."

There is no mistaking this creature who is called the great dragon, for he is marked out with great detail. His fingerprints are put down here in the Revelation. Because God knew that a great percentage of the preachers of this century would teach that Satan does not exist, He makes it so you cannot miss him. If your enemy can get you to think he does not exist, he will have a tremendous advantage over you, and he will be able to get a crack at you that will sweep you off your feet. Satan moved in afresh and anew during my generation simply because my generation did not believe in him. Now we are getting an overdose of him, and he has been made a weird and wild thing. But, actually, he is not an ugly creature, by any means; he is an angel of light.

Notice how he is identified here:

1. He is called "the old serpent." This takes us back to the Garden of Eden. Our Lord said, ". . . He was a murderer from the

beginning . . ." (John 8:44). The words *old* and *beginning* are akin, according to Vincent. Satan is that old serpent, the one who was at the beginning in the Garden of Eden.

2. He is called "Devil," a name which comes from the Greek *diabolos*, meaning "slanderer or accuser." He is so labeled in verse 10: "the accuser of our brethren." This is the reason believers need an Advocate with the Father. You and I have an enemy today who is not only causing us problems down here, but you would be surprised what he says about you and me in heaven! There is nothing that you do or say or think which he does not turn in against you up yonder. But God already knows about it, and I like to beat Satan to the draw and confess it before he gets up there to bring the accusation against me. The Lord Jesus is our Advocate. "My little children, these things write I unto you, that ye sin not. And if any man sin, we have an advocate with the Father, Jesus Christ the righteous" (1 John 2:1).

It would be wonderful if I did not sin, but I do. Thank God that we have an Advocate with the Father. Jesus Christ the righteous is up there to defend us. He has been kept busy ever since I have been in this world, and I have a notion He's been pretty busy defending you, too. Don't think He is up there sitting idly by. He is our Defender, our Advocate. The Devil is a slanderer; he is a liar from the beginning. He is the origin of all lies today. Where does the gossip that goes on in some of our churches originate? It originates in the pit of hell, my friend. That is the last place from which anything ought to be shipped into the church!

3. He is also called "Satan," which means "adversary." He is the awful adversary of God and of every one of God's children. We are told: "Be sober, be vigilant; because your adversary the devil, as a roaring lion, walketh about, seeking whom he may devour" (1 Pet. 5:8). I have received a great many letters from people who have been delivered out of cults and "isms" through the study of the Word of God. One man wrote: "I was in a cult. I wrote you the letter I did [and it was a mean one!] to try to trap you, to try to trick you. I thought I was right and you were wrong. When I began to study the Word of God, I came to realize how Satan had trapped me." Satan has a lot of folk trapped today, even church members. We need to recognize that he is

our enemy. That does not mean we should go overboard and just dwell on Satan and demons. It certainly is true that there is a new and fresh manifestation of him today that was not here a generation ago. But keep your eye on Jesus Christ, for He is your place of deliverance, and He is up yonder to help you.

4. Finally, he is called "he that deceiveth the whole (inhabited) world." During the Great Tribulation, Satan will be able to *totally* deceive men—today he deceives only partially. Satan deceives men relative to God and the Word of God. He caused Eve to distrust God: "Has God said you should not eat of that tree? You just can't trust Him, can you?" (see Gen. 3:1–4). Satan deceives man relative to man. Satan makes out mankind better than he is, yet he despises us. He builds us up and tells us we could become gods—how wonderful that would be (see Gen. 3:5). Satan deceives man relative to the world, the flesh, and the Devil. You and I think we are big enough to overcome the world, the flesh, and the Devil, but we are not big enough to overcome any *one* of them. The world is too big for us, and it will certainly draw us away from the Lord. Satan deceives man relative to the gospel. He does not mind a man going to church or even joining a dozen churches, but he does not want that man to be saved. "In whom the god of this world hath blinded the minds of them which believe not, lest the light of the glorious gospel of Christ, who is the image of God, should shine unto them" (2 Cor. 4:4).

Someone has said, "Satan is to be dreaded as a lion; more to be dreaded as a serpent; and most to be dreaded as an angel." That is where he traps the multitude today.

And I heard a loud voice saying in heaven, Now is come salvation, and strength, and the kingdom of our God, and the power of his Christ: for the accuser of our brethren is cast down, which accused them before our God day and night.

And they overcame him by the blood of the Lamb, and by the word of their testimony; and they loved not their lives unto the death.

> **Therefore rejoice, ye heavens, and ye that dwell in them. Woe to the inhabiters of the earth and of the sea! for the devil is come down unto you, having great wrath, because he knoweth that he hath but a short time [Rev. 12:10–12].**

> *And I heard a great voice in heaven saying, Now is come the salvation, and the power, and the kingdom of our God, and the authority* [Gr.: *exousia*] *of His Christ; for the accuser of our brethren is cast down, the one accusing them before our God day and night. And they overcame him because of the blood of the Lamb, and because of the word of their testimony; and they loved not their life even until death. Therefore, rejoice, O heavens, and ye that dwell in them. Woe for the earth and for the sea; because the devil is gone down unto you, having great wrath, knowing that he has but a short time.*

"And I heard." This reminds us that John is still the spectator and auditor of these events. He does not want us to forget that, because it is very important.

When Satan has been cast out of heaven, it will cause great rejoicing among the redeemed who are in heaven. "A great voice in heaven" seems to refer to the Old Testament saints or to the Tribulation saints who have been martyred up to this point (see Rev. 6:9–10), for they mention their brethren on the earth: "for the accuser of our brethren is cast down."

The first great demonstration of power to be exerted against evil after the death and resurrection of Christ is the casting out of Satan from heaven. That is the beginning of the movement that will lead to the Lord Jesus taking over the reins of government down here. When Christ died on the cross, He paved the way for Satan's being cast out of heaven. Listen to the language in Colossians: "Blotting out the handwriting of ordinances that was against us, which was contrary to us, and took it out of the way, nailing it to his cross" (Col. 2:14). The Lord Jesus made it possible for man to be saved by His death. God canceled our debt of sin by nailing it to the cross of Christ. Christ made full payment. Paul goes on to say: "And having spoiled principalities and powers, he made a shew of them openly, triumphing over them in it" (Col. 2:15). I personally believe that this began when He ascended into heaven and took that great company of saints with Him. He led captivity captive and took them into the presence of God. Those were the Old Testament saints, and I think they are in this group who are now saying that salvation is come.

This opens the way for the coming of four great, blood-bought, heavenly freedoms. We talk about four freedoms down here which have not yet come to pass, but here are four freedoms that are going to come to pass when Christ comes.

1. "The salvation"—its consummation is in the person of Christ. Our salvation will not be consummated until we are in His presence: "Beloved, now are we the sons of God, and it doth not yet appear what we shall be: but we know that, when he shall appear, we shall be like him; for we shall see him as he is" (1 John 3:2). This will be true when He comes to the earth. I believe this verse speaks of His visible return to the earth.

2. "The power." The way nations have handled power has been tragic. This has been true of every great nation. Some nations have been able to make war and, like a great prairie fire, they have spread across another nation, destroying cities and killing people. The nations have abused power, but it will be wonderful when Christ takes the power and controls this earth.

3. "And the kingdom of our God" is going to be established on the earth. Not until then will there be peace and righteousness and freedom on this earth. In this land of the free and home of the brave, there are not many brave left, and I don't know that there are many free who are left either. It will be wonderful when His kingdom comes on this earth. This very statement reveals that the kingdom was not established at the first coming of Christ.

4. "And the authority (Gr.: *exousia*) of His Christ" shows that Christ has not yet taken over the governmental authority of this world. He is not building a kingdom; He is not establishing His kingdom today. Wait until He starts moving. All of these judgments are in prep-

aration for His return to this earth, giving men a warning and an opportunity to turn to Him—and multitudes will do so. There is always a note of grace in the judgment of God.

"The one accusing them before our God day and night" reveals that this is part of the present strategy of Satan which attempts to thwart Christ's purpose with His church today and with the Tribulation saints tomorrow. This necessitates Christ's present ministry as Advocate for us.

Victory for the accused saints comes through three avenues which are mentioned to us in this section:

1. "The blood of the Lamb." There is wonder-working power in the blood of the Lamb. Don't you forget that. Let us not minimize that. The many references to the blood of the Lamb necessitate its being on display in heaven. This is not a crude conception; rather, the crudity is in our sins which made it necessary for Him to shed His blood. If you and I get any victory, it will be because He shed His blood for us. We will never, never be able to lead "the victorious life." The most defeated people I have ever met have been people who are supposedly living "the victorious life." All of them look anemic to me. They look to me like they are fugitives from a blood bank. They are shallow and sallow looking, and they need a blood transfusion. *They* don't live a victorious life—*Christ* does! If any of us overcome, it will be through the blood of the Lamb.

2. "The word of their testimony" reveals that they were true martyrs. Those who are Christ's cannot deny Him. "But whosoever shall deny me before men, him will I also deny before my Father which is in heaven" (Matt. 10:33). There is something that is strengthening in giving a testimony. Don't misunderstand me—some of the testimonies given today are pretty shallow. Some of them are given by those who ought not to be giving a testimony, because the people close to them know their shoddy living, and it makes them rather cynical and skeptical. The place to give a testimony is not at a nice, well-fed church banquet where all the saints say amen to everything you say. If you have a life to back it up, the place to give your testimony is out yonder in the world, when you are up against that

godless, blaspheming crowd. Let them know that you belong to Christ and that you are in Christ. There is something strengthening in that. There is something that makes a man stand tall when he can give a testimony like that. I know of a man in business who is a big, double-fisted fellow. He is an executive in a very hard-hitting concern, and there are a lot of blaspheming folk around him. When he hears someone blaspheming, in a very quiet manner, he will say to that person, "I'd like to tell you what Jesus Christ means to me." The Lord Jesus says, "If you deny Me before men, I'll deny you before My Father in heaven" (see Matt. 10:33). These are the true martyrs. The Greek word *martus* means "witness." These are the ones who witness for Him.

3. "They loved not their life even unto death." This is an exalted plane to come to, where you and I make the Lord Jesus the first love in our life and put love of self down in second, third, fourth, or some other place. Surely we ought to have respect for ourselves, and there ought to be a dignity about us, but let's put Him first. When we put Him first, we will not have any problem living for Him down here. The great problem today is not the set of rules you may be living by; it is what is behind the rules. Here is what you need behind them: the blood of the Lamb, the word of your testimony, and love for Him above everything else. Love is the very basis of service. The Lord said to Simon Peter, "Do you love me?" When Simon Peter finally could say that he did, although on a weak plane, the Lord Jesus said, "I am going to use you. You are going to feed My sheep" (see John 21:15–17). Peter preached the first sermon in the church and probably saw more people saved per capita of those then living than any other time in the history of the world.

There are two radical reactions to the casting out of Satan from heaven. There is rejoicing in heaven, for this awesome, treacherous, dangerous, and deadly serpent is out forever. Then there is woe on the earth. This is the third woe that extends through the pouring out of the seven bowls of wrath. The only consolation for the earth is that Satan's sojourn on earth is brief—forty-two months. There is an intensification of tribulation during this period.

THE DRAGON PERSECUTES THE WOMAN

And when the dragon saw that he was cast unto the earth, he persecuted the woman which brought forth the man child.

And to the woman were given two wings of a great eagle, that she might fly into the wilderness, into her place, where she is nourished for a time, and times, and half a time, from the face of the serpent [Rev. 12:13–14].

This is the last wave of anti-Semitism that will roll over the world, and it is the worst, because Satan is cast down to the earth and knows that his time is short. He hates Israel because Christ came from this nation according to the flesh. This is the Time of Jacob's Trouble, and this is the reason I cannot rejoice in the present return of Israel to that land. Some people seem to think they are going back for the Millennium. They are not—they are going back for the Great Tribulation Period if they are going back for any purpose at all, according to the Word of God.

"Two wings of a great eagle" are given to her that she might fly into the wilderness. There are those who see in this the airplane that will take Israel to their hiding place, and they always pick the rock-hewn city of Petra as being that place. I do not know how an airplane would land in that place, but that is the problem of those who give that explanation.

"Two wings of a great eagle" is not something that is unusual or peculiar to the people of Israel, but it is reminiscent of the grace of God in His past deliverance of Israel from Egypt. He said to them: "Ye have seen what I did unto the Egyptians, and how I bare you on eagles' wings, and brought you unto myself" (Exod. 19:4). They had not come out of Egypt by their own effort or their own ability. They came out because God brought them out, and eagles' wings became a symbol to them. Here again in the Great Tribulation, the Israelites cannot deliver themselves, and no one is interested in delivering them. But God will get them out on eagles' wings by His grace.

"Into the wilderness, into her place." Scripture does not say that the rock-hewn city of Petra will be that place. It could be, but we just simply do not know. This "wilderness" has been variously identified—Petra is not the only place. Some say that it is the wilderness of the peoples of the world; that is, that there will be another worldwide scattering of Israel. Since Christ said, ". . . flee into the mountains" (Matt. 24:16), we believe it to be a literal wilderness, possibly that same one in which Israel spent forty years under Moses. This time it will be forty-two months, for that is the meaning of "a time, and times, and half a time." The important thing is not the place but the fact that God will protect them by His grace.

"Where she is nourished" reminds us that in the past God sustained them with manna from heaven and water from the rock. He will nourish them again in possibly the same way.

And the serpent cast out of his mouth water as a flood after the woman, that he might cause her to be carried away of the flood.

And the earth helped the woman, and the earth opened her mouth, and swallowed up the flood which the dragon cast out of his mouth [Rev. 12:15–16].

And the serpent cast out of his mouth after the woman water as a river, that he might cause her to be carried away by the stream. And the earth helped the woman, and the earth opened her mouth and swallowed up the river which the dragon cast out of his mouth.

In view of the fact that the wilderness is literal, the water also could be literal. God had delivered Israel out of the water, both at the beginning of the wilderness march at the Red Sea and then again at the end of the wilderness march at the Jordan River. However, the floods of water could be armies flowing like a river upon them. This figure of speech has been used by Isaiah (see Isa. 8:7–8).

In Ezekiel's picture of the last days, the king of the north is seen marching on Israel. Satan will use every means to destroy the people.

How will he be stopped? No nation is there to stop him. But God is there, and He will destroy him with natural forces when he invades Palestine: "And I will plead against him with pestilence and with blood; and I will rain upon him, and upon his bands, and upon the many people that are with him, an overflowing rain, and great hailstones, fire, and brimstone" (Ezek. 38:22). This gives us an indication of what John is talking about here in Revelation.

THE REMNANT OF ISRAEL

And the dragon was wroth with the woman, and went to make war with the remnant of her seed, which keep the commandments of God, and have the testimony of Jesus Christ [Rev. 12:17].

And the dragon was wroth with the woman, and he went away to make war with the rest of her seed, that keep the commandments of God and hold the testimony of Jesus.

"The rest of her seed" may refer to the remnant who is God's witness in this period—the 144,000 who have been sealed. They are evidently witnessing throughout the world. These "keep the commandments of God," which places them back under the Law. This precludes the possibility of the witnesses being the church.

All anti-Semitism is Satan inspired and will finally culminate in Satan's making a supreme effort to destroy the nation of Israel. From the brickyards of Pharaoh's Egypt, Haman's gallows, Herod's cruel edict, through Hitler's purge, and to the world of the Great Tribulation, Satan has led the attack against these people because of the Man Child—Jesus Christ.

CHAPTER 13

THEME: *Wild beast out of the sea and earth*

Seven personages are introduced to us by the seventh trumpet, five of whom we met in chapter 12: the woman, or Israel; the red dragon, Satan; the child of the woman, Christ; Michael, the archangel; and the remnant of Israel, that is, the 144,000 who were sealed of God and who are going to make it through the Great Tribulation. In chapter 13 the final two personages are brought before us. One is the wild Beast out of the sea; he is both a political power and a person. The other is the wild Beast out of the earth; he is a religious leader. Here is where the action is when we come to these personages. Here is revealed to us the great warfare that is going on between light and darkness, between God and Satan. It is manifested now as we draw to the end of the age during the Great Tribulation Period.

These two Beasts are presented to us as *wild* beasts—that is the literal translation. It is bad enough to be a beast, but to be a wild beast compounds the injury. There is much disagreement among reputable Bible expositors as to the identity of the Beasts. Some consider the first beast to be a person, while others treat him as the last form of the Roman Empire. Some treat the second Beast as the Man of Sin, while others consider him merely as the prophet, or the John-the-Baptist type, for the first Beast. These difficulties arise because it is impossible to separate a king from his kingdom. A dictator must have a realm over which he rules, or he is no dictator. Though it is difficult to distinguish the two, it seems that the first beast is the antichrist, the ruler over the restored Roman Empire. In Revelation 16:10 it speaks of "the throne of the wild beast." I would judge from this that there is somebody to sit on that throne, and that is the Beast who is presented here—but he would not be the Beast if he did not have the empire. After determining the identity of the first Beast, it is not really difficult to identify the second. He is a man, the false prophet, the religious leader, who leads in the worship of the first Beast—and he is antichrist also.

There is another view being held today that antichrist is the denial of the person of Christ rather than an actual person. In other words, antichrist is false doctrine rather than a person yet to be revealed. The explanation, I believe, is found in the meaning of the preposition *anti*, which has two usages. The first maenaing of *anti* is "over against." Its second meaning is "instead of" or "in place of." It has both meanings in Scripture. In both his first and second epistles, John mentions the antichrist. He is the only one who uses that designation. We can see both of these characteristics in antichrist; he is the one who is *against* Christ and the one who *imitates* Christ—antichrist is both.

In his first epistle John writes: "Little children, it is the last time: and as ye have heard that antichrist shall come, even now are there many antichrists; whereby we know that it is the last time" (1 John 2:18). "Little children, it is the last time." John said that nineteen hundred years ago. We have been in the last time a long time! Note here that John not only says there is going to be an antichrist, but that already in his day there were *many* antichrists. What was the thing which identified an antichrist? "Who is a liar but he that denieth that Jesus is the Christ? He is antichrist, that denieth the Father and the Son" (1 John 2:22). Antichrist denies the deity of Christ. He is against Christ. He is *the* enemy of Christ on the earth.

In the fourth chapter of his first epistle, John tells us some additional facts concerning antichrist. "Beloved, believe not every spirit, but try the spirits whether they are of God: because many false prophets are gone out into the world. . . . And every spirit that confesseth not that Jesus Christ is come in the flesh is not of God: and this is that spirit of antichrist, whereof ye have heard that it should come; and even now already is it in the world" (1 John 4:1, 3). In other words, any person or any group or any book that denies the deity of Christ is antichrist. I consider the rock opera, *Jesus Christ Superstar*, to be antichrist. It is against the Jesus Christ of the Bible. Also, any minister who denies the deity of Christ is antichrist—he is *against* Christ.

In John's second epistle we read: "For many deceivers are entered into the world, who confess not that Jesus Christ is come in the flesh. This is a deceiver and an antichrist" (2 John 7). Antichrist is a deceiver—he *pretends* to be Christ, and he is not. The Lord Jesus Christ said, "There are going to be many who will come in My name, saying, 'I am Christ.' You are to test them because not every spirit is of God." We need to test the spirits today. My friend, you need to start by testing your little group or the cult in which you are interested. Instead of being super-duper saints, they may actually be following an antichrist. Our Lord warned of such in the Olivet Discourse: "For there shall arise false Christs, and false prophets, and shall shew great signs and wonders; insomuch that, if it were possible, they shall deceive the very elect" (Matt. 24:24). There will arise false Christs who will be able to perform miracles; this second Beast is really a miracle worker—he is an antichrist.

Therefore, the first Beast is political Antichrist, and the second Beast is religious Antichrist. Even the Devil cannot put it all together in one person. I believe there are two persons, these two Beasts, who are antichrist.

WILD BEAST OUT OF THE SEA—DESCRIPTION, A POLITICAL POWER AND A PERSON

The first verse of this chapter introduces the Beast from the sea.

> **And I stood upon the sand of the sea, and saw a beast rise up out of the sea, having seven heads and ten horns, and upon his horns ten crowns, and upon his heads the name of blasphemy [Rev. 13:1].**

Let me give you my translation:

> *And he stood on the sand of the sea; and I saw a (wild) beast coming up out of the sea, having ten horns and seven heads, and on his horns ten diadems, and upon his hands names of blasphemy.*

My translation reads, "And *he* stood on the sand of the sea," but the Authorized Version reads, "And *I* stood upon the sand of the sea," as if it were John. The better manuscripts today show the subject of the sentence to be *he*. Who is he? Whom were we last talking about in the previous chapter? He is the same person, and that, of course, is Satan.

"And I saw a (wild) beast coming up out of the sea." Who brings him out of the sea? Satan brings him out of the sea. In Scripture the sea is a picture of the nations of the world, of mankind, like the restless sea.

"Having ten horns and seven heads, and on his horns ten diadems, and upon his heads names of blasphemy." This Beast really boggles the mind. If I were to meet him in the dark, I know for sure that he and I would be going in the same direction, only I would be *lots* farther down the road than he would be!

The dragon (Satan) stands on the sands of the sea, and it is he who brings the wild Beast out of the sea and dominates him. This is Satan's masterpiece. The first Beast is a person who heads up the old Roman Empire. Rome simply fell apart, and this is the only one who will ever be able to put it together again.

God is apparently taking His hands off this earth for awhile and turning it over to Satan. I believe this is poetic justice. God must let Satan demonstrate that, when he is given full sway, he will not be able to produce. Otherwise, Satan would always be able to say to God from the lake of fire, "You never gave me a chance. If You would have taken Your hands off and let me alone, I would have been able to accomplish my purpose and establish a second kingdom." But God is going to let Satan have his way so that he will not be able to say that.

An understanding of the prophecy of Daniel is very important to the understanding of the Revelation. This wild Beast is similar in description to the fourth beast, that nondescript beast, in the seventh chapter of Daniel. There it represents the prophetic history of the Roman Empire, down to "the little horn" and his destruction. That fourth beast looked like it became dormant for a little while, and then out of one of its seven heads there came up ten horns, out of which came a little horn. The little horn put together three of the horns and was able to take the other seven.

At the time of the writing of John, much of the prophecy of Daniel had been fulfilled. The first three beasts—Babylon, the lion; Media-Persia, the bear; and Graeco-Macedonia, the panther—had all been fulfilled. When Daniel gave it, it was prophecy, but it was fulfilled by John's time. Therefore, John centers on the fourth beast and upon the little horn because the fourth beast, the Roman Empire, had appeared. John was living in the time of the Roman Empire, having been exiled to the Isle of Patmos by the Roman emperor, Domitian. Already, signs of weakness and decay were visible in the empire, and John was spectator to that which was still future in Daniel's day. However, in the Book of Revelation the emphasis is upon the rule of the little horn of Daniel 7, and the little horn is set before us as a wild Beast, for he is now ruling and controlling the restored Roman Empire in John's prophecy. The little horn of Daniel 7 and the wild Beast of Revelation 13 are identical. You can see that an understanding of Daniel 7 would be basic to understanding this passage.

The wild Beast is the Man of Sin and Antichrist, the final world dictator. The last verse of this chapter confirms this view. "Here is wisdom. Let him that hath understanding count the number of the beast: for it is the number of a man; and his number is Six hundred threescore and six" (v. 18). We are dealing with the man who is the world dictator at the end.

There has been a great deal of excitement in our day (and I am included in the group that is excited) about the current existence of the Common Market in Europe. Throughout history, there have been many who have attempted to put Europe back together again. Charlemagne attempted it and failed. I think that the Roman Catholic church attempted it in the Holy Roman Empire and certainly did not succeed. The Holy Roman Empire was centered in Vienna, Austria, which makes it a very interesting place to visit today. Franz Josef was the last of the emperors of the Holy Roman Empire who tried to put Europe together, but he was the worst flop of all. His son apparently either was murdered or committed suicide, and that ended the Holy Roman Empire. Napoleon, Kaiser Wilhelm, Hitler, and Mussolini all attempted it. But God has not been ready yet, and He will not let that one appear until the time of the Great Tribulation. To me the Common

Market is interesting, not because we are seeing prophecy fulfilled, but because we are seeing the stage set which reveals that prophecy *can* be fulfilled. Down through the centuries, many have said that it is impossible to get Europe together. It *is* impossible until God is ready—and Satan is going to supply the man. The Common Market is just an interesting instrument—that's all.

The ten horns with ten diadems speak of the tenfold division of the Roman Empire in the time of the Great Tribulation. The horns are the ten kings who rule over this tenfold division. This interpretation is confirmed by Revelation 17:12.

The little horn comes to power by first putting down three of these rulers, and afterward he dominates the other seven and thus becomes the world dictator.

The seven heads are not so easily identified. They are interpreted in Revelation 17:9–10 as seven kings. These do not reign contemporaneously as the ten horns do, but they appear in chronological order. Some have interpreted them as representing certain Roman emperors, such as Domitian who was then ruling. Others interpret these seven heads as the forms of government through which the Roman Empire passed. They had kings, councils, dictators, decemvirs, military tribunes, and emperors. The third view is that the seven heads could represent seven great nations of antiquity which blasphemed God: Rome, Greece, Media-Persia, Chaldea, Egypt, and Assyria. The kingdom of the Beast which is yet to come would be the seventh. Another likely view is that the seven heads correspond to the seven heads of the dragon which denote exceptional wisdom. Satan energizes the Man of Sin, the last dictator. I cannot be dogmatic about any one of these views and do not feel that it is crucial to do so.

All seven heads are guilty of blasphemy. Blasphemy manifests itself in two ways according to Govett: (1) making oneself equal with God, that is, usurping His place, and (2) slandering and taking God's name in vain. The emperors of Rome were guilty of the first form. They made themselves equal with God; there was emperor worship in the Roman Empire. The Pharisees were guilty of the latter when they blasphemed the Holy Spirit. The Beast here is guilty of both forms.

And the beast which I saw was like unto a leopard, and his feet were as the feet of a bear, and his mouth as the mouth of a lion: and the dragon gave him his power, and his seat, and great authority [Rev. 13:2].

And the wild beast which I saw was like unto a panther, and his feet were as the feet of a bear, and his mouth as the mouth of a lion: and the dragon gave him his power, and his throne, and great authority.

This is really a weird-looking creature! He has never been seen on land or sea or in the air. Without doubt, this is a real spectacle.

John notes that he is a composite Beast. We can begin now to formulate some very definite facts concerning Antichrist. He combines the characteristics of the other beasts representing kingdoms which Daniel saw in his vision of Daniel 7. Consulting that passage and my commentary on the Book of Daniel might be helpful to you at this point.

(a) "And the wild beast which I saw was like unto a panther." The outward appearance of the Beast was like a panther: "After this I beheld, and lo another, like a leopard, which had upon the back of it four wings of a fowl; the beast had also four heads; and dominion was given to it" (Dan. 7:6). *Panther* and *leopard* are the same Greek word; I prefer the word *panther*. This was the Graeco-Macedonian Empire. Greece was noted for its brilliance and its advancement in the arts and sciences. It was noted for its philosophy, its architecture, and its marvelous literature. The Greek language itself is a wonderful language. The empire of the Beast will have all the outward culture which was the glory of Greece.

(b) "And his feet were as the feet of a bear" reminds us of the second beast of Daniel: "And behold another beast, a second, like to a bear, and it raised up itself on one side, and it had three ribs in the mouth of it between the teeth of it: and they said thus unto it, Arise, devour much flesh" (Dan. 7:5). This was Media-Persia, noted for its pagan splendor as it paddled and waddled over the earth like a

Gargantua. The empire of the Beast will have all the pagan splendor and wealth that Media-Persia had.

(c) "And his mouth as the mouth of a lion" reminds us of the first beast of Daniel: "The first was like a lion, and had eagle's wings: I beheld till the wings thereof were plucked, and it was lifted up from the earth, and made stand upon the feet as a man, and a man's heart was given to it" (Dan. 7:4). This was Babylonian autocracy. When Nebuchadnezzar ordered the death of his wise men and then later on the fiery furnace for the three Hebrew children, there was none to question his authority. He was the head of gold; he was an autocrat. Though the Man of Sin will be one of the toes of the image that Daniel saw, composed partly of clay and partly of iron, he will rule with the autocracy and dictatorial authority of Nebuchadnezzar.

This final world dictator comes to his zenith under the domination of Satan. The source of his power is found in Satan who raises him up, empowers and energizes him for the dastardly dictatorial job he will do. He is the closest to an incarnation of Satan that appears in Scripture. Luke said that Satan had entered into Judas Iscariot (see Luke 22:3). Christ used similar language when He spoke to Simon Peter in Matthew 16:23. Is the Man of Sin the incarnation of Satan? I think we can say that he is. Certainly Satan has entered into him. Paul wrote: "Even him, whose coming is after the working of Satan with all power and signs and lying wonders, And with all deceivableness of unrighteousness in them that perish; because they received not the love of the truth, that they might be saved" (2 Thess. 2:9–10).

WILD BEAST, DEATH-DEALING STROKE

And I saw one of his heads as it were wounded to death; and his deadly wound was healed: and all the world wondered after the beast [Rev. 13:3].

And I saw one of his heads as though it had been slain unto death; and his stroke of death was healed; and the whole (inhabited) earth wondered after the beast.

This verse, together with chapter 17, verse 8, has led many to the view that Satan actually raises the Beast from the dead. "The beast that thou sawest was, and is not; and shall ascend out of the bottomless pit, and go into perdition: and they that dwell on the earth shall wonder, whose names were not written in the book of life from the foundation of the world, when they behold the beast that was, and is not, and yet is" (Rev. 17:8).

Because of these two Scriptures, there are many who have taken the position that the Beast is actually raised from the dead by Satan. This cannot be because Satan does not have power to raise the dead; that power has not been given to him at all. The Lord Jesus Christ is the only One who can raise the dead. The Gospel of John records these words spoken by our Lord: "For as the Father raiseth up the dead, and quickeneth them; even so the Son quickeneth whom he will. . . . Verily, verily, I say unto you, The hour is coming, and now is, when the dead shall hear the voice of the Son of God: and they that hear shall live. . . . Marvel not at this: for the hour is coming, in which all that are in the graves shall hear his voice, and shall come forth; they that have done good, unto the resurrection of life; and they that have done evil, unto the resurrection of damnation" (John 5:21, 25, 28–29). Only the Lord Jesus can raise the dead—Satan cannot. Therefore, I take it that the restoration is a false, a fake resurrection.

Those who take the view that Satan raises the Beast from the dead interpret the Beast as a man only. That the early church, for the most part, held to this view is indisputable. They disagreed as to the identity of the Beast. Some thought he was Judas Iscariot. Others identified him as Nero. Even Augustine, in his day, wrote:

> What means the declaration, that the mystery of iniquity doth already work? Some suppose it to be spoken of the Roman Emperor, and therefore Paul did not speak in plain words, although he always expected that what he said would be understood as applying to Nero, whose doings already appeared like those of Antichrist. Hence it was that some sus-

> pected that he would rise from the dead as Antichrist [J. A. Seiss, *The Apocalypse, Lectures on the Book of Revelation*, p. 398, footnote].

There are others who take the view that the Beast here refers to the Roman Empire and that the imperial form of government, under which Rome fell, will be restored in a startling manner. I believe this will happen, but I do not think it is a resurrection, for Rome never died; Rome fell apart. Rome is like Humpty-Dumpty:

> Humpty-Dumpty sat on a wall;
> Humpty-Dumpty had a great fall;
> All the King's horses, and all the King's men
> Could not put Humpty-Dumpty together again.

But Antichrist can and will put Humpty-Dumpty together again, and it will be a marvelous thing. The Roman Empire has not truly died; it lives on in the nations of Europe today.

I think that both of these views do have something to commend them, while both views have serious objections. There can be no real resurrection of an evil man before the Great White Throne judgment. And, at that time, only Christ can raise the dead. Christ will raise the dead who stand before the Great White Throne (see Rev. 20:11–15). We have already considered John 5:28–29: "Marvel not at this: for the hour is coming, in the which all that are in the graves shall hear his voice, And shall come forth; they that have done good, unto the resurrection of life; and they that have done evil, unto the resurrection of damnation." Only Christ can rise the dead—both saved and lost. Satan has no power to raise the dead. He is not a life-giver. He is a devil, a destroyer, a death-dealer.

The Roman Empire is to be revitalized and made to cohere in a miraculous manner under the world dictator, the beast, yet verse 3 seems to demand a more adequate explanation than this.

I believe the beast is a man who will exhibit a counterfeit and imitation resurrection. This will be the great delusion, the big lie of the Great Tribulation Period. We are told that God will give them over to believe the big lie (see 2 Thess. 2:11), and this is part of the big lie. They will not accept the resurrection of Christ, but they sure are going to fake the resurrection of Antichrist.

"And his stroke of death was healed" shows the blasphemous imitation of the death and resurrection of Christ. The challenge in that day will be: "What has Christ done that Antichrist has not done?" Nobody can duplicate the resurrection of Christ; they might imitate it, but they cannot duplicate it. Yet Antichrist is going to imitate it in a way that will fool the world—it is the big lie. Believers say, "Christ is risen!" The boast of unbelievers in that day will be: "So is Antichrist!" The Roman Empire will spring back into existence under the cruel hand of a man who faked a resurrection, and a gullible world who rejected Christ will finally be taken in by this forgery.

We begin now to get a composite picture of the Antichrist. The rider on the white horse (see Rev. 6) brought a false peace to the world. In the recorded history of man, he has engaged in fifteen hundred wars and has signed some eight thousand peace treaties. Yet in his entire history, he has enjoyed only between two and three hundred years of true peace. Certainly G. K. Chesterton was accurate when he said, "One of the paradoxes of this age is that this is the age of Pacifism, but not the age of Peace." The Antichrist comes in on a false platform of bringing peace to the world. How many times in the United States have we elected a president on the platform that he would bring peace, only to find that he took us right into a war? We have been a warlike nation. We are not very peaceful.

Arnold Toynbee, an English historian, said this in 1953:

> By forcing on mankind more and more lethal weapons, and at the same time making the world more and more interdependent economically, technology has brought mankind to such a degree of distress that we are ripe for deifying any new caesar who might succeed in bringing the world unity and peace.

That is all Antichrist will need to offer the world when he comes. He will say, "I am going to give you peace," and the people will say "Hallelujah!" and put him into office. That is the way we do it in the

United States where we are supposed to be a very cultured, educated, sophisticated, and civilized nation. The world will put Antichrist into power.

Bishop Fulton J. Sheen made this remarkable statement:

> The Antichrist will come disguised as the great humanitarian. He will talk peace, prosperity, and plenty, not as a means to lead us to God, but as ends in themselves. He will explain guilt away psychologically, make men shrink in shame if their fellowmen say they are not broad-minded and liberal. He will spread the lie that men will never be better until they make society better.

This is one statement made by Bishop Sheen which I'll agree with one hundred percent.

WILD BEAST, DEITY ASSUMED

And they worshipped the dragon which gave power unto the beast: and they worshipped the beast, saying, Who is like unto the beast? who is able to make war with him? [Rev. 13:4].

And they worshipped the dragon, because he gave his authority unto the beast; and they worshipped the beast, saying, Who is like unto the beast? and who is able to make war with him?

This is the supreme moment for Satan. He wants to be worshiped, and the whole world is going to worship him during this period. My friend, if the Spirit of God took His hand off this world today and off you and me, I am afraid that many of us would be in the position of backsliders; and if Antichrist appeared, we would follow him like a little faithful dog follows his master.

"And they worshiped the beast, saying, Who is like unto the

beast?" What a parody on the worship of the true God. They say, "Look, we are worshiping something more wonderful than the God of the Bible!"

> **And there was given unto him a mouth speaking great things and blasphemies; and power was given unto him to continue forty and two months [Rev. 13:5].**
>
> *And there was given to him a mouth speaking great things and blasphemies; and there was given to him authority to continue (to work) forty and two months.*

The only good news here is that Antichrist will be reigning like this for only forty-two months, or three and one-half years.

"A mouth speaking great things" means he is a big-mouthed fellow. Daniel also mentions this concerning him. He is really going to be a big talker; he will promise anything. This is one reason you ought to be careful listening to anyone on radio or television today, including this poor preacher or any politician or educator or newsman. We need to test everything that we hear. Antichrist is going to have charisma. He is going to be able to talk himself into the good graces of this Christ-rejecting world.

WILD BEAST, DEFYING GOD

> **And he opened his mouth in blasphemy against God, to blaspheme his name, and his tabernacle, and them that dwell in heaven [Rev. 13:6].**
>
> *And he opened his mouth for blasphemies against God, to blaspheme His name and His tabernacle and those which dwell (tabernacle) in heaven.*

This is the dreadful limit to which the Beast goes in blasphemy. He is against Christ and His church which are in heaven. Thank God that the church is no longer on the earth! I do not see how anyone who studies Revelation can believe that the church is going to go through this period of the Great Tribulation.

> **And it was given unto him to make war with the saints, and to overcome them: and power was given him over all kindreds, and tongues, and nations.**
>
> **And all that dwell upon the earth shall worship him, whose names are not written in the book of life of the Lamb slain from the foundation of the world [Rev. 13:7–8].**
>
> *And it was given unto him to make war with the saints and to overcome them: and there was given to him authority over every tribe and people and tongue and nation. And all that dwell on the earth shall worship him, every one whose name hath not been written from the foundation of the world in the book of life of the Lamb that hath been slain.*

"And it was given unto him to make war with the saints." The saints (there will be saints during the Tribulation Period, although they are not, of course, the church) will be overcome by the brutal Beast. In the will of God many believers, both Jew and Gentile, will suffer martyrdom.

"And all that dwell on the earth shall worship him, every one whose name hath not been written from the foundation of the world in the book of life of the Lamb that hath been slain." Spurgeon used to say something like this: "I am glad that my name was written in the Lamb's Book of Life before I got here, because if God had waited until I got here, He never would have chosen me." That is true of all the saints, both in the church age and in the Great Tribulation Period.

This will be the darkest hour in the history of the world; and the church, thank God, will not be here. I am thankful I am not going through the Great Tribulation Period. I will not be under Antichrist; I am under Christ. I am not looking for Antichrist; I am looking for Christ to come.

WILD BEAST, DEFIANCE DENIED TO ANYONE

If any man have an ear, let him hear.

He that leadeth into captivity shall go into captivity: he that killeth with the sword must be killed with the sword. Here is the patience and the faith of the saints [Rev. 13:9–10].

If any man hath an ear, let him hear. If any one is for captivity (bring together captives) into captivity he goeth (away): if any man shall kill with the sword, with the sword must he be killed. Here is the patience and the faith of the saints.

This is without doubt one of the most awe-inspiring statements in the Word of God. "If any man" is a thrice-repeated invitation to the ear of anyone to hear the Word of God at any time, in any age. "So then faith cometh by hearing, and hearing by the word of God" (Rom. 10:17). "If any man hath an ear, let him hear." Here again is the wedding of free will and election. "If any man"—any man means *any* man. "If any man hath an ear"—does not everybody have ears? Yes, but there are some people who do not hear although they have ears. There are people who simply do not listen at all—they do not hear.

I had a neighbor who was retired, and his wife was a very wonderful person, but she talked a great deal. When he would go outside to work, he would remove his hearing aid from his ear. He did it, I discovered, for a purpose. He was pruning a tree one day when his wife came out of the house and talked a blue streak to him for about five minutes. All of a sudden she noticed that he did not have his hearing aid on. She said, "You haven't heard a word I've said!" He just kept on sawing, and she turned around and went back into the house. That was exactly what he wanted! He was out there to prune the tree and not to carry on a conversation.

There are a great many people who do not have a hearing aid to hear the Word of God—they don't want to hear it. I would like to make it possible for every person in this country to study the Word of God with us through our radio Bible studies. But I do not have the wildest dream that *everybody* in the country is going to be studying the Word of God. I know that it will be only those who have an ear, an ear to hear the Word of God. "Any man"—that's free will; that "hath an ear" is election; and this is the way God weds these two truths together.

"He that leadeth into captivity shall go into captivity: he that killeth with the sword must be killed with the sword." What John is saying here is not for you and me—at least, I hope it is not for you; I know it is not for me—because, beginning with chapter 4, Revelation is dealing with future things which are beyond the church. The church (meaning all born-again believers in this age) will no longer be on earth. John is speaking to God's saints who will be in the world at that time. Remember that during the Tribulation the Antichrist will be the world dictator. Men are not going to buy or sell without his permission. They will not be able to travel without his permission. He will rule the world as no one has ever ruled in the past. God is saying to those who are His own, "Don't resist him." To begin with, it would not do you any good. The second thing is that this is "the patience and the faith of the saints" of that time. If you are in the world during the Great Tribulation, then you are going to have to bear with patience and faith the awful trials that will be coming even upon God's children.

God will apparently withdraw from the world, and He will turn it over to Satan. Today the Holy Spirit is in the world, and He curtails, He smothers, resistance. He is holding back evil, although it may not look that way. Just think what it will be like when He is removed from that office and when evil men are permitted to have their day. Satan will have full sway. As we have said before, this actually is poetic justice. The Devil and his minions of evil and lost mankind will never be able to say to God, "You never gave us a chance. If You had just given us a chance, we would have been able to work things out." God is going to give them a chance for a brief period. If it was not for just a brief period, there would be no flesh left on the earth, as the Lord Jesus said (see Matt. 24:22).

THE WILD BEAST OUT OF THE EARTH— DESCRIPTION, A RELIGIOUS LEADER

The first Beast is a political leader, a political power and a person, and his power will become worldwide. We come now to the second wild Beast, the one who comes out of the earth and is a religious leader.

> **And I beheld another beast coming up out of the earth; and he had two horns like a lamb, and he spake as a dragon [Rev. 13:11].**
>
> *And I saw another wild beast coming up out of the earth and he had two horns like a lamb, and he was speaking as a dragon.*

This wild Beast is easier to identify than was the first. After you establish who the first Beast is it is not too much trouble to identify the second. The first Beast comes out of the sea, and the second one comes out of the earth. What is the difference? The sea represents the peoples of the world. The great mob of mankind today is like the surging and restless sea—that has always been true. The earth from which this second Beast arises is symbolic of Palestine, and it is naturally assumed that the second Beast comes from Israel. He is a messiah, and Israel would not accept him unless he had come from their land and was one of them.

"And he had two horns like a lamb." This suggests his imitation of Christ. The first Beast is *opposed* to Christ—he is *Anti*christ. The second Beast *imitates* Christ. He also is *Anti*christ (considering *anti*, meaning "instead of"); he poses as Christ. He has two horns like a lamb, but he is a wolf in sheep's clothing. He imitates the ". . . Lamb of God, which taketh away the sin of the world" (John 1:29), only this pseudolamb does not subtract sin; he adds and multiplies it in the world. He does not come to do his own will, but the will of the first Beast. He is a counterfeit Christ. He will do a lot of talking about loving everyone, but underneath he is a dangerous Beast, just as the first one was, deceiving the whole world.

The Lord Jesus said in Matthew 7:15: "Beware of false prophets, which come to you in sheep's clothing, but inwardly they are ravening wolves." This second Beast is the epitome of all false prophets, and he is an Antichrist. It takes two men to fulfill the position that Christ fulfills—and of course, they do *not* fulfill it. But Satan needs two men to attempt even an imitation of Him.

Again, the Lord Jesus said in Matthew 24:24: "For there shall arise false Christs, and false prophets, and shall shew great signs and wonders; insomuch that, if it were possible, they shall deceive the very elect." The false prophet is sort of a "John the Baptist" to the first Beast. Some have identified him as King Saul or Judas, which is mere assumption and cannot be proved.

WILD BEAST, DELEGATED AUTHORITY

And he exerciseth all the power of the first beast before him, and causeth the earth and them which dwell therein to worship the first beast, whose deadly wound was healed [Rev. 13:12].

And he exerciseth all the authority of the first wild beast in his presence. And he maketh the earth and the dwellers therein to worship the first wild beast, whose wound of death was healed.

The second wild Beast has a delegated authority from the first wild Beast, which actually makes him subservient to him, but he is also on a par with him—he has the same power.

This second wild Beast leads in a movement to exterminate the harlot of Revelation 17, which is the false church that will go into the Great Tribulation Period. John does not even dignify that church by calling it a church; it is called a harlot. The true church, which has now left the earth, is called the bride of Christ. But here you have the last vestige of an apostate church with all of its humanism. The false prophet will offer the world something new to worship—the first wild Beast, the willful king, the Man of Sin, the last world dictator (see Dan. 11:36–39; Matt. 24:24; 2 Thess. 2:3–10). Here is presented to us this terrible second Beast who will exalt the first Beast to the place of worship.

"Whose wound of death was healed" reveals that both the first and the second Beasts are healers and miracle workers. This is the big lie, the "strong delusion" that is going to come to the world.

> **And he doeth great wonders, so that he maketh fire come down from heaven on the earth in the sight of men,**
>
> **And deceiveth them that dwell on the earth by the means of those miracles which he had power to do in the sight of the beast; saying to them that dwell on the earth, that they should make an image to the beast, which had the wound by a sword, and did live [Rev. 13:13–14].**
>
> *And he doeth great signs, that he should even make fire to come down out of heaven into the earth in the sight of men. And he deceiveth the dwellers on the earth through [Gr.: dia] the signs which it was given him to do in the presence of the wild beast; saying to the dwellers on the earth that they should make an image [Gr.: eikon] to the beast who hath the stroke of the sword and lived.*

This false prophet is a worker of signs and miracles (see Matt. 24:24). Our Lord warned against this false prophet. His deception is that he apes Elijah in bringing down fire from heaven. He is a combination of Jannes and Jambres: "Then Pharaoh also called the wise men and the sorcerers: now the magicians of Egypt, they also did in like manner with their enchantments. For they cast down every man his rod, and they became serpents: but Aaron's rod swallowed up their rods" (Exod. 7:11–12). In other words, they were clever magicians, and I believe they had satanic power. This Beast in the end time will also have satanic power.

We read in Matthew 3:11: "I indeed baptize you with water unto repentance: but he that cometh after me is mightier than I, whose shoes I am not worthy to bear: he shall baptize you with the Holy Ghost, and with fire." John the Baptist specifically said he had nothing to do with fire, but this false prophet is going to imitate Elijah.

The false prophet plays with fire until he is cast into the lake of fire (see Rev. 19:20). The world is taken in by this deception, with the exception of God's elect, those who are His—they *cannot* be deceived.

The false prophet shows his hand by causing to be made an image of the man of sin. The Greek word for image is *eikon*, which means "likeness." The big production is a likeness of the first Beast that emphasizes the wound of death that was healed. It is interesting to note that the Lord Jesus did not permit anything connected with His physical appearance to survive. But the likeness of the Antichrist will evidently be placed in the temple at Jerusalem, and I believe it is the abomination of desolation to which our Lord referred: "When ye therefore shall see the abomination of desolation, spoken of by Daniel the prophet, stand in the holy place, (whoso readeth, let him understand:)" (Matt. 24:15). This is the abomination of desolation that is to appear, and although we cannot be dogmatic, we believe it will be this image of Antichrist, the first wild Beast.

WILD BEAST, DELUSION PERPETRATED ON THE WORLD

And he had power to give life unto the image of the beast, that the image of the beast should both speak, and cause that as many as would not worship the image of the beast should be killed.

And he causeth all, both small and great, rich and poor, free and bond, to receive a mark in their right hand, or in their foreheads:

And that no man might buy or sell, save he that had the mark, or the name of the beast, or the number of his name [Rev. 13:15–17].

And it was given to him to give breath [Gr.: *pneuma*] *to the image of the wild beast, that the image of the wild beast should both speak, and cause that as many as should not worship the image of the beast should be killed. And he causeth all, the small and the great, and the rich and the poor, and the free and the slave, that there be given them a mark on their right hand or upon their forehead; and that no one should be able to buy or to sell, except the one having the mark, even the name of the beast or the number of his name.*

"And it was given to him to give breath (the Greek word is *pneuma*) to the image of the wild beast." This is going to be a different kind of idol. Isaiah and all the prophets mention the fact that idols cannot speak. Paul also mentions it. But here is an idol that will speak. I think they will call all the scientists of the world to look at this image. The scientists will give a report that they cannot understand it, they cannot explain it and that it is a miracle. This is something that will cause the whole world to turn and worship the Beast.

He is now wedding religion and business, for you will have to have the mark of the Beast to do business. In John's day soldiers were branded by their commanders, slaves were branded by their masters, and those attached to certain pagan temples were branded by the mark of the god or goddess whom they served. Ptolemy Philopater had all Jews in Alexandria marked with the ivy leaf, which was the symbol of Dionysus. In our day a newspaper columnist who wrote an article entitled, "Living by the Numbers," deplored the fact that we have to carry so many different cards in our wallets and concluded with this paragraph:

> It would simplify matters if the government would assign each of us a single all-purpose number which we would have tattooed across the forehead to spare us the trouble of carrying all these cards.

Don't misunderstand me. This is *not* the fulfillment of prophecy, but it sure shows how prophecy *can* come to pass. What is the mark of the Beast? It is not given us to know. We are not told, but that has not kept many expositors from telling us what it is!

WILD BEAST, DESIGNATION

Here is wisdom. Let him that hath understanding count the number of the beast: for it is the number of a man; and his number is Six hundred threescore and six [Rev. 13:18].

Here is wisdom. He that hath understanding, let him count the number of the beast; for it is the number of man; and his number is six hundred and sixty and six.

"Here is wisdom" seems to be a rather ironical declaration when we consider the maze of speculation that has been accumulated through the centuries on this verse.

In the Greek there is a very beautiful arrangement of this number.

hexakosioi — 600
hexekonta — 60
hex — 6

A numerical value is attached to each letter to be sure, but we must let it stand there, for the visible number of the Beast and its meaning await the day of his manifestation. And I do not believe he has yet been manifested. This number has made a nice little jigsaw puzzle for a lot of people to play at, but, my friend, you will not know who he is until you get to the Great Tribulation Period.

I would suggest that we not waste our time trying to identify a person by this number. Instead, we need to present Jesus Christ that we might reduce the population of those who have to go through the Great Tribulation Period and who will therefore know what the number of the Beast is.

I am not anxious to know the number of the Beast, and I am thankful I will not have to live in that period. I am very thankful today that I know Jesus Christ as my Savior. Instead of spending time with Antichrist, I want to know Christ. I can say with Paul: "That I may know him, and the power of his resurrection, and the fellowship of his sufferings, being made conformable unto his death" (Phil. 3:10).

The only positive and important item for us today is that the first beast is a man. This teaches me not to trust man. "Thus saith the LORD; Cursed be the man that trusteth in man, and maketh flesh his arm, and whose heart departeth from the LORD. For he shall be like the heath in the desert, and shall not see when good cometh; but shall inhabit the parched places in the wilderness, in a salt land and not inhabited. Blessed is the man that trusteth in the LORD, and whose hope the LORD is. For he shall be as a tree planted by the waters, and that spreadeth out her roots by the river, and shall not see when heat cometh, but her leaf shall be green; and shall not be careful in the year of drought, neither shall cease from yielding fruit" (Jer. 17:5–8).

The passage in Revelation does not interest me a bit as to what the number of the Beast is or who he is or anything about him, but it makes me want to know Jesus Christ more, because my plan is to be with Him—not because of who I am or what I have done, but because Jesus Christ died for me on the cross, and by His grace I will go into His presence.

BIBLIOGRAPHY

(Recommended for Further Study)

Barnhouse, Donald Grey. *Revelation, an Expository Commentary*. Grand Rapids, Michigan: Zondervan Publishing House, 1971.

Criswell, W. A. *Expository Sermons on Revelation*. Grand Rapids, Michigan: Zondervan Publishing House, 1966.

Epp, Theodore H. *Practical Studies in Revelation*. Lincoln, Nebraska: Back to the Bible Broadcast, 1969.

Gaebelein, Arno C. *The Revelation*. Neptune, New Jersey: Loizeaux Brothers, 1915.

Hoyt, Herman A. *The Revelation of the Lord Jesus Christ*. Winona Lake, Indiana: Brethren Missionary Herald, 1966.

Ironside, H. A. *Lectures on the Book of Revelation*. Neptune, New Jersey: Loizeaux Brothers, 1960. (Especially good for young converts.)

Larkin, Clarence. *The Book of Revelation*. Philadelphia, Pennsylvania: Published by the author, 1919. (Includes fine charts.)

Lindsey, Hal. *There's a New World Coming*. Santa Ana, California: Vision House Publishers, 1973.

McGee, J. Vernon. *Reveling Through Revelation*. 2 vols. Pasadena, California: Thru the Bible Books, 1962.

Newell, William R. *The Book of Revelation*. Chicago, Illinois: Moody Press, 1935.

Phillips, John. *Exploring Revelation*. Chicago, Illinois: Moody Press, 1974.

Ryrie, Charles C. *Revelation*. Chicago, Illinois: Moody Press, 1968. (A fine, inexpensive survey.)

Scott, Walter. *Exposition of the Revelation of Jesus Christ*. London: Pickering and Inglis, n.d.

Seiss, J. A. *The Apocalypse, Lectures on the Book of Revelation*. Grand Rapids, Michigan: Zondervan Publishing House, 1957.

Smith, J. B. *A Revelation of Jesus Christ*. Scottsdale, Pennsylvania: Herald Press, 1961.

Strauss, Lehman. *The Book of Revelation*. Neptune, New Jersey: Loizeaux Brothers, 1964.

Walvoord, John F. *The Revelation of Jesus Christ*. Chicago, Illinois: Moody Press, 1966. (Excellent comprehensive treatment.)